WHAT WOULD Henry DO?

Essays for the 21st Century

Dedicated to the residents of Concord and
to the Town of Concord, our partners in
preserving the birthplace of Henry David Thoreau

Thoreau Farm Trust board at the birth house, June 2017
(left to right) Jack Maguire, Ken Lizotte, Molly Eberle,
Nancy McJennett, Joseph C. Wheeler
Absent from photo: Deborah Bier, Court Booth, Lawrence Buell

BIRTHPLACE OF HENRY DAVID THOREAU
(1817-2017) 200TH BIRTHDAY

Direct all correspondence to:

Thoreau Farm Trust, Inc.
341 Virginia Road, Concord, MA 01742
email: info@thoreaufarm.org
www.thoreaufarm.org

Contents

Photo credit: Rich Morgan Photography

Ken Lizotte, CMC, is President of the Board of Trustees at Thoreau Farm and Chief Imaginative Officer (CIO) and founder of emerson consulting group inc. Author of seven books, Ken lives in Concord with his wife Barbara, daughter Chloe, and Golden Retriever Beckett.

Introduction:
What Would Henry
Think, Say, and Do?

Ken Lizotte

When Henry David Thoreau was born on July 12, 1817, a rather
static world had begun to change. Societies in every corner of
the earth had long been dominated by agriculture, ensuring a life
where most everyone remained in one place from birth to death,
living on and working off the land just outside one's door. You
interacted with the same friends and neighbors day in and day
out, you thought the same thoughts, adhered to the same credos,
held similar assumptions.

Yet as Henry grew and matured in his little hometown of
Concord, Massachusetts, the world around him seemed to break
into pieces. Suddenly, or so it seemed, an age-old accepted
socioeconomic system — slavery — came under fire, to the point
where many of Henry's friends and acquaintances were willing
to risk imprisonment in order to aid perfect strangers trying to
escape bondage hundreds of miles to the south.

Just as suddenly, blind patriotism no longer held sway for
many native-born Americans, who viewed the outbreak of war
with Mexico as unjust and important enough to resist. Again,
imprisonment and social ostracism were potential repercussions.

During the same period, technology began to infringe upon
people's expectations in a manner that upended the very basis for
how they spent their days. Trains now transported large groups
of individuals every day to workplaces 20-30 miles away, hauling

them back at night to their homes for dinner and a night's sleep before resuming the process the very next morning. For many, toiling all day on the family farm was no longer their only option.

For Henry and others, such upheavals both confused and disconcerted, raising questions that for centuries most individuals had never had to face: What should I think about these times? What should I say about these times? And what, if anything, should I do about them?

Today, on the same little planet, we, too, live in bewildering times. We're essentially faced with the same questions: What should we be thinking, saying, and doing about the challenges bearing down upon us? What should we think, say, and do about (for example) climate change, governmental intrusion, the potential for nuclear war, toxic waste, or polluted water? How about the ever-escalating costs of higher education, or of healthcare, or of food and shelter? And what of terrorism, attacks on our freedoms, hackers, poverty, and hate crimes?

Answers that will truly solve such crises can be hard to come by, and even harder when seeking answers that everyone can agree upon. But we, the community of Thoreau Farm, believe we have to try. For that reason, it was natural for us to wonder, if Henry were alive today, what would *he* think, what *he* say, what would *he* do?

The result is this collection of many of today's great thinkers who chose to ponder these questions, especially the last one, by speculating how Henry might respond. We invite you to enjoy this volume, contemplate its messages, and conjure up a few of your own.

Feature Essay

by President Jimmy Carter

Photo credit: The Carter Center

Jimmy Carter was the 39th President of the United States (1977-1981). In 2002, Mr. Carter was awarded the Nobel Peace Prize "for his decades of untiring effort to find peaceful solutions to international conflicts, to advance democracy and human rights, and to promote economic and social development."

What Would Henry David Thoreau Do?

Jimmy Carter

Having read much of Thoreau's writing and having visited Walden Pond, I can understand how different were the threats to our environment 170 years ago.

Global warming was first detected when I was president, by scientists at Woods Hole Oceanographic Institution in Massachusetts, and I was both skeptical and alarmed by their report. It was a few years later that human activity was found to be the cause of the increase in temperature. This is one of the most serious threats to our planet (along with nuclear weapons), and I am sure that Thoreau would be deeply concerned and personally active in combatting these problems.

Not being averse to civil resistance, he would probably be in the forefront of activists, as well as a prolific writer and debater on the public stage. His major weapon would be the logic of his exhortations, and he would be prolific with his explanations of how deterioration of our environment would affect the average person in our society. His emphasis would likely be on the poorest among us being the first victims, as he defended those who were enslaved during his lifetime.

Feature Essay

by Joseph C. Wheeler

President Jimmy Carter (left) shakes hands at the White House in 1979 with Joseph C. Wheeler, USAID Assistant Administrator for the Near East during Carter's administration.

Joseph C. Wheeler is the fourth son of dairy farmers Caleb and Ruth Wheeler. He was born on Thoreau Farm and educated in the Concord schools, Bowdoin College, Graduate Institute of International Studies in Geneva, and Harvard's Littauer Center of Public Administration.

Capping a forty-year career, he served in 1980-1982 as Deputy Administrator of The United States Agency for International Development. He later served as Deputy Executive Director of The United Nations Environment program, Chairman of the Development Assistance Committee of the OECD (DAC), and as a senior staff member preparing for the 1992 Rio United Nations Earth Summit on Environment and Development.

After retiring in Concord, Wheeler served on a number of boards related to population and food production. He served on Concord's Historical Commission, as a board member of the Thoreau Society, and as the first president of the Thoreau Farm Trust, which preserved and maintains the home in which Henry David Thoreau was born.

Bringing Henry David Thoreau Up to Date

Joseph C. Wheeler

By some magic, I was recently returned to Concord in my 200th birth year for a brief tour. I met Joe Wheeler, who updated me on the past 155 years since I moved to Concord's Sleepy Hollow Cemetery in 1862.

We first went to my birthplace on Virginia Road, the old Wheeler-Minot Farmhouse, now called Thoreau Farm, which was moved up the street in 1878. Much to my surprise, the house has been preserved by a group of local citizens with help from the Town.

Eight months after my birth in 1817, we left Thoreau Farm. A volcano that erupted in Indonesia in 1815 might have been responsible for our moving. It left so much ash in the air that it changed the weather around the world in 1816-17. Historians call 1816 "The year without a summer," with frosts in New England in July. No wonder my father felt unsuccessful as a farmer, and moved on to other pursuits.

Joe told me that he was a distant cousin of mine.

Joe's mother came from Watertown, like my grandmother, Mary Jones Dunbar-Minot. Joe had a story about his Watertown grandfather, G. Frederick Robinson, who liked to camp out at Fairhaven Bay, and liked it so much that he bought a lot and built a camp to spend summers in Concord. Thus it was no surprise that when his daughter Ruth grew up, she met and married a local farm boy named Caleb Wheeler. They purchased property on Virginia Road and called it Thoreau Farm.

Later, Ruth Wheeler became a local historian, and in 1941, helped to form The Thoreau Society, which holds a meeting every year close to my birthday, so I can't complain that I've been forgotten. Joe claims that he was born in the same airspace that I was, since the house that replaced my family's home was built on the same foundation. Surprisingly, the farm is now completely wooded, like most of Concord, since farming has declined.

Walden Pond is now a state park, and people still go swimming there, take rambles, and visit the site of my cabin. Fairhaven Woods and lots of other land in Concord have been preserved, especially by The Concord Land Conservation Trust. As one who advocated for the preservation of land for the enjoyment of nature, I must say I was very pleased to hear of these measures.

Joe says the big issues of today are managing the atomic bomb and dealing with global warming. The problem seems to be that we've had a very rapid series of technical innovations. When I moved to Sleepy Hollow, we had already invented the steam locomotive, the railroad, and telegraph. Then around 1900 came the automobile (which quickly took the place of horse and carriage). Then the airplane, which enables one to get to England in a few hours. To my amazement, there have been several revolutions in communications: the telephone, radio, television, and digital systems.

We have gone from wood to coal to oil to natural gas. Now there is a movement to replace these earth-warming fuels with energy in the form of electricity from solar panels, windmills and who knows what else. They have even put solar panels at my birth house, partly because they figured I would have approved such a move, which I certainly do.

In Concord we now have three primary schools (named for the Alcotts, Simon Willard and, believe it or not, for me), and we have two middle schools and a huge high school shared with Carlisle. Joe told me he has a good friend whose daughter entered high school last year, and her first big project was to develop a collection of leaves. This project got the young woman to take a ramble or two and learn to identify over 50 different kinds of trees. Also, scientists now point to my journals to track when birds migrated and flowers first bloomed in the spring.

They even have a course at high school called Rivers and Revolutions, which is described by its founder as exploring the writings of Aldo Leopold and Annie Dillard; canoeing the Concord River; examining the development of early civilizations along floodplains; strolling through Minuteman National Historical Park; contemplating the relationship of circles and lines; hiking across glacial deposits; and reveling in the waters of Walden Pond. That is my kind of education!

In 1862, Concord was a farming town. We were famous for asparagus, strawberries, apples, and milk. In 2017, there are no milking cows left, and only a few farms. The biggest industry is the hospital.

I miss the blacksmiths.

Feature Essay

by Margaret Carroll-Bergman

Margaret Carroll-Bergman is the executive director of Thoreau Farm. She lives in a 575-square-foot cabin on White Pond with her husband and two dogs. Their adult children visit in shifts.

Thoreau Farm: Birthplace of Henry David Thoreau, Birthplace of Ideas

Margaret Carroll-Bergman

"(I was) born July 12, 1817 in the Minott House, on the Virginia Road..."
— Henry David Thoreau

While Concord holds its place in history as the birthplace of the famous 19th century Transcendentalist community, Henry David Thoreau was the only member who was born right here in Concord.

This year, 2017, is the bicentennial anniversary of Henry David's birth. If Henry were alive today, I think he would be pleased that his birthplace is preserved as a source of inspiration for living deliberately, practicing simplicity, and exploring new ideas for positive change.

Henry's parents, John and Cynthia, lived at what is now called Thoreau Farm from 1813 through 1818. His maternal grandmother Mary Minot* was widowed and had remarried, and upon the death of her second husband, Jonas Minot, received a "widow's third" of Minot's estate. Henry's grandmother then asked her daughter and son-in-law to move to Virginia Road and manage her share of the estate.

When Henry David — born "David Henry," an order he reversed later in life — was eight months old, the Thoreaus gave up the farm. Yet Henry David had a great sense of life on the farm, as Cynthia often spoke of what it was like growing up there.

"My mother was telling tonight of the sounds which she
used to hear summer nights when she was young and
lived on Virginia Road — the lowing of the cows or
cackling of geese, or the beating of a drum as far off as
Hildreth's but above all Joe Meriam whistling to his team,
for he was an admirable whistler. Says she used to get up
at midnight and go and sit on the door-step when all in
the house were asleep and she could hear nothing in the
world but the ticking of the clock in the house behind her."
— *Journal* of Henry D. Thoreau, May 26, 1857

One can still experience solitude and a similar pastoral setting
today while visiting Thoreau Farm. It's a perfect place to pack a
picnic, walk the grounds, and pull out a journal, sketchpad, or
book. At Thoreau Farm, you can still hear sounds that Cynthia
and Henry David would have heard — birds calling in the trees
in spring, the quiet rattle of wind in winter, the rustle of autumn
leaves, and the damping of sound that only a blanket of snow
can cause.

Perhaps known best for *Walden* and his meditations on solitude,
Henry David also thrived on intellectual discourse with his
Transcendentalist peers. Today, you can experience that same
community and fellowship by attending diverse events and
programs, most held in the birthplace meeting room.

Whether you are attending an author's talk, taking a guided tour,
or walking around the grounds, you can be sure you'll run into
fellow Thoreauvians doing the same.

The birthplace has been preserved to look just the way it did in
1817. Yet the renovation incorporates many green technologies,
including roofing shingles and siding made from recycled
material; solar-powered electricity to run the heating and air-
conditioning; composting toilets; green building materials, stains
and paints; and a barrel to collect rainwater to irrigate the kitchen
garden. Henry David Thoreau, viewed as the father of the
modern environmental movement, would most likely approve of

the recycling, repurposing, and reusing of materials during the course of the renovation of his family's first home.

After the family left in 1818, Thoreau's birthplace underwent many changes in ownership. In 1878, it was relocated from 215 to 341 Virginia Road, which was the eastern end of the farm. During this move, the central chimney and a lean-to addition were demolished to make it easier to move the house a quarter-mile or so down Virginia Road. Various architectural alternations over the years followed this move.

Despite such an uprooting and physical transfer, and substantive physical changes to the house in the two centuries since, it seems fitting that the home has remained in many ways basically the same, especially as regards the room where Henry David was born. I like to think he would appreciate that his birth room appears all but untouched these many years later.

It should be noted however that, instead of a cradle, rocking chair, and a bed to re-create a nursery, the trustees of Thoreau Farm chose to remake Henry's birth room into a place of quiet contemplation and reflection, the better to honor this particular baby's legacy. Quotes from Thoreau's writings line the wall, as well as pictures of world leaders influenced by his ideas, and members of the Thoreau nuclear family. Henry's birth room doubles as a writer's retreat, available to rent by the hour, day, week, or month, in keeping with the Thoreau Farm Trust's vision of Henry's first home as an active and continuous "birthplace of ideas."

Many writers and visitors who have spent time in this Thoreauvian writer's retreat report that they have literally felt a "presence," typically described as kind and supportive, and always, at the least, invigorating and productive. Perhaps, this might be Henry returning to encourage Thoreau Farm's writer-visitors to (as he once advised) "Write while the heat is in you!" And so they do!

The last owner to farm the property was James Breen, Jr., who died in 1995. Two years later, the town acquired the land, and a group of citizen activists came together to establish the current non-profit Thoreau Farm Trust to carry out a mission of preserving Henry's birthplace and to use it for ongoing educational programs that advance Thoreau's teachings, now and forever. In 2004, the house was listed in the National Register of Historic Places, and in 2007, the Town of Concord officially transferred the farmhouse and its two-acre lot to Thoreau Farm Trust.

Please note that Thoreau Farm depends on donations from people like you, those who wish to help keep Henry's legacy alive. Visit www.thoreaufarm.org and subscribe to an e-list to receive notifications of upcoming events and programs, and learn how you can support and join Thoreau Farm.

*The different spellings of the Minot family and the Minott House, though referring to the same family, are not typos, but a result of differing spellings in historical references.

Photo credit: PeterAldenwildlife.com

Peter Alden is a world-renowned naturalist, lecturer, and ecotourism guide based in Concord. He is author of 15 books on North American and African wildlife, including the National Audubon Society's Regional Field Guide Series.

Henry's Focus on Nature

Peter Alden

Happy 200th birthday up there. The Thoreau Society and Thoreau Farm run programs from your birth house today. You and your writings are known by millions. You have inspired many people to be observers and activists, and are regarded as the father of a new discipline, environmentalism. Your curiosity and respect for the natural world in your hometown and region are greatly admired. As an environmentalist and ecologist, I would like to update you on the ups and downs of the habitats, plants, and animals today in your cherished Concord.

In the mid 1800s, Concord and most of New England was a sea of cattle pastures, grasslands, organic field crops and orchards. Open-country birds such as kestrels, bobolinks, meadowlarks, and field sparrows were everywhere. Today those fields are mostly replaced with homes and returning forests, and those field birds are scarce.

Woodlots were small, scattered, and valued chiefly for firewood in the 1800s. Today, much of Concord is covered with forests, thanks to federal, state, and town actions, in addition to private groups like the Concord Land Conservation Trust.

You would be impressed with the number and variety of mammals now present in Concord. Hunted out in your day, the white-tailed deer has returned big time and numbers in the hundreds in town. With the lack of large carnivores and so much land closed to hunting, deer have become a threat to many native wildflowers.

Beavers are flourishing and have created ponds in many places. The resultant dead trees have allowed colonies of great blue herons to spring up. Moose and black bears wander through town, while bobcats, fishers, and porcupines are again residents. Opossums from the south and coyotes from the west have joined them. We've lost the New England cottontail (replaced by eastern cottontails), and our bats are declining.

The wild pigeon trappers of your day are gone because the passenger pigeon, once the world's commonest bird, is now extinct! However, wild turkeys, which you never saw, have been successfully introduced by the Mass. Dept. of Fisheries and Wildlife. Concord is now home to several hundred. Spectacular pileated woodpeckers, shot out in your day, are again common. Canada geese, strictly migrants in the 1800s, are now full-time residents and a bit of a nuisance. Osprey, bald eagles, and ravens now nest nearby, due to decades of protection.

A number of "southern birds" like the red-bellied woodpecker and Carolina wren have expanded their ranges northwards since your day. Climate change, due to massive worldwide consumption of coal, petroleum and natural gas, invasive plant fruits, and the new craze of bird feeding are all factors.

Amongst the reptiles, the snapping and painted turtles remain common, the same with garter and water snakes. The wood and box turtles have become rare, while great effort is made locally to protect a disjunctive population of Blanding's turtle. Frogs and salamanders are doing quite well due to laws protecting vernal pools.

Pollinators, such as honeybees and some bumblebees, are declining. Overuse of dangerous pesticides is a concern. Outbreaks of the caterpillars of Asian gypsy moths and European winter moths skeletonize the leaves of our forest and ornamental trees.

Your contributions to local botany were enormous. Your records of average first flowering times of local wildflowers over many years have been replicated recently. Scientists from Boston University can now show that flowering is about ten days earlier. Your data of simultaneous arrival dates for returning songbirds, when compared with today's data, reveals that similar changes have occurred. Such historical data cannot be recreated by the strongest computers in the world!

About 20% or so of the wildflowers you were tracking have vanished from Concord due to deer overgrazing, habitat changes, and other factors. We have also gained a number of "new" plants overrunning various ecosystems in town.

Field weeds have been a challenge for farmers for centuries. In the last few decades, several dozen horticultural trees, shrubs, vines and herbs have escaped from gardens and are overwhelming native plants. Most have pretty leaves, flowers or fruit for a few weeks, but are ecological disasters. Problem trees include Norway maple and black locust. Oriental bittersweet, porcelain berry and black swallow-wort are draping over and killing native plants. Our meadows and watersides are now flush with invasive purple loosestrife and Old World common reed.

It is fascinating to see these changes and I wonder what you, Henry, would do and say if you could see them too.

Billy Anderson grew up on Hubbard Street in Concord at a remarkable time, and joined his family of shopkeepers on the Milldam at Anderson Photography across from Anderson Market. Selling photography at that time was also teaching photography. His grandmother was a passionate Thoreauvian photographer, who became Billy's great influence as a result of her talent for seeing nature through her photograph lens.

Illustrating Thoreau and Nature

William Wheeler Anderson

My grandmother Esther Wheeler grew up on a family farm in the Nine Acre Corner section of Concord and took up picture-taking around 1930. When N.C. Wyeth published *Men of Concord* in 1936, my grandmother began writing a journal, which she called *Travels around Concord on Horseback.* She wrote in the manner of Thoreau, recording what she saw, though without Thoreau's philosophical view of life.

To fully assume Thoreau's process of walking on a daily basis, as my grandmother did, you begin to understand the Transcendentalists and their walks in Concord. It is one of the most genial landscapes one can ever experience amidst the dry pine forest and the fragrant river atmosphere. How different it is today, where people sit in vehicles and careen through space and time, completely oblivious to Thoreau's methodology.

Thoreau would have adhered to his methodology, consistent throughout his short life: to saunter daily along the village pathways and byways while recording what he saw and thought. His time was always spent on foot hereabouts and on his writing, which proved as thorough as any man or woman who ever wrote. Thoreau's Journal, for example, is a masterpiece of thought and observation. Today, he would almost certainly be using a camera as well.

Henry would frequently depart to saunter under the noon sun, returning with the setting sun warming his back. While traveling, he would be watching for the emergence of descendants of flowers where he had found them in previous years. Esther

Wheeler found that her pictures duplicated many of Thoreau's observations, and that was a meeting of their minds.

In 1941, when The Thoreau Society was organized, Esther Wheeler gave the Society a slide lecture of her pictures, now preserved in book form as *Thoreau Country*, and accompanied it with Thoreau quotes. The new Kodachromes were spectacular, especially when projected in a dark living room in winter, the greens of summer in particular exploding into view!

I have been excited to learn of N.C. Wyeth's interest in Concord, as the vast Fairhaven Woods, the very wood lots Thoreau and Eddy Hoar set ablaze, almost certainly were preserved as a result of his influence. Wyeth was obsessed with Thoreau's philosophy, so much so that for many years his greatest challenge was to create pictures for a book filled with Thoreau's writing. A frequent visitor to Concord, he stayed in the home of Mrs. Helen Wright on Fairhaven Bay, sister of Ruth Wheeler, well before his book was published. Incidentally, his son Andrew Wyeth was born on Thoreau's 100th birthday, and so would be 100 this July if he had lived.

Just as Wyeth was inspired to illustrate Thoreau's *Men of Concord*, Esther Wheeler was inspired to use her photographs to illustrate the timeless rural nature of Concord found in the writing of Thoreau, who once declared: "The scenery when it is truly seen, reacts on the life of the seer... That is my everyday business."

And so Thoreau's works continue to instill passion in artists today.

Photo credit: Ed Begley, Jr.

Ed Begley, Jr. is an actor and an environmentalist.

Happy Birthday, Henry!

Ed Begley, Jr.

In lieu of a birthday cake with candles (an odd custom you would abhor), we have chosen to light up our atmosphere with climate change, then while making a wish for a higher GDP, extinguish countless plant and animal species that were around in your day.

But it's not all bad news.

You can watch your favorite reality show on a device that you can hold in one hand while you elect your favorite reality star to the highest office in the land with the other.

Just to bring you up to speed, the natural world that you so revered hit a real low in the late 60s ... the 1960s!

We had horrible air pollution in most of our cities, and rivers catching fire outside Cleveland.

The very symbol of our nation, the bald eagle, was headed for extinction.

But then a crazy thing happened ... we actually started to make things better, with incredible leadership from both Republicans and Democrats!

We passed something called the Clean Air Act, the Clean Water Act, and the Endangered Species Act, after which things actually started to improve on several fronts.

Even though we had four times the cars, and millions more people in cities like Los Angeles, the air didn't get worse ... it didn't stay the same ... it got better ... much better!

The Cuyahoga River didn't catch fire any more. The Hudson River, so polluted you couldn't eat the fish, likewise made a miraculous recovery. Something called the Ozone Hole got really bad, then got a lot better after we passed laws to deal with that.

We started to move aggressively away from coal and other dirty fuels, and move towards cleaner power like solar panels and wind turbines. Come to think of it, since you never used electricity, those two might not be high on your list, but think of the Dutch using windmills to do a job.

These cleaner companies started to hire a lot of people, with benefits and fair wages.

Folks realized that the cost of not addressing a lot of these problems like dirty air and polluted water was quite high. It simply made good economic sense to fix them.

And it wasn't just the environment that got better. Folks started to be more tolerant of people who looked or acted different than them. As an abolitionist, you'd be proud, I know, of how far we came on that front. We actually elected our first black president … twice!

Using your principles of civil disobedience, we just kept making things better and better.

Then, a really sad thing happened. A lot of good folks (who got left out in the cold by both parties) aligned themselves with a group that wanted to go back to a "better" time (but no, not a simple life in a cabin near Walden Pond).

They aligned themselves with a group that had little regard for protecting nature. They were all friends of, or actually heads of, extractive industries that made things so bad in the 60s — the same kinds of industries that made life so difficult in the cities that you avoided when you returned to Walden Woods.

At the hands of our new leadership, we find ourselves headed down a dangerous path, a path where little regard is given to the web of life that supports us all. And by that I mean the plant and animal species that you studied and catalogued at Walden, and many more around the globe.

And, having made great progress being tolerant of others, we headed to a dark and angry time, where many folks became less tolerant of those that we perceived as "others."

But then another thing happened. Once again, using your principles of civil disobedience, folks started to take to the streets again. They became more informed, more active as citizens, and stood up for what they believed in.

The final chapter of this struggle has not been written yet. I suppose it never will, but it's probably fitting that it's all playing out on what would be your 200th birthday.

I intend to find a nice spot in a relatively intact part of the world to celebrate your life and legacy, and I promise I won't add to the problem with so much as a candle!

Keith Bergman is a career municipal manager in Massachusetts. The Bergmans live in Concord on White Pond — "a lesser twin of Walden," Thoreau wrote.

Editor's note: Keith is a volunteer with The Climate Reality Project, a global network of activists committed to tackling the climate crisis, founded by former Vice President Al Gore. He was one of the first fifty trained by Mr. Gore to present the slideshow on climate change featured in the film, "An Inconvenient Truth." Thoreau Farm invited Keith to present an updated version of that slideshow on Earth Day 2017 as part of our celebration of Henry's 200th birthday.

Environmentalism and Activism

Keith Bergman

There is a direct line from Henry David Thoreau's writings on environmentalism and activism in the 19th century to the greatest challenge facing America in the 21st — combating climate change during the Trump administration's assault on science.

Henry David's sublime appreciation for the natural world in *Walden* is the bedrock upon which the modern environmental movement was built, just as his "Civil Disobedience" informed both Mahatma Gandhi and Martin Luther King, Jr., and gave birth to non-violent protest.

Some parallels to Thoreau's day and ours are disturbing. "Civil Disobedience" was published in 1849; *Walden* in 1854. That decade also gave rise to the Know-Nothings, a party opposed to new immigrants, their minority religion, and the jobs lost by the majority.

Know-Nothing 2.0 in the Trumpian Age not only targets immigrants, religion, and jobs, but does so with a misplaced pride in actually knowing nothing. No facts. No science. No soul. No concern for the future of the planet.

To weather this storm in current political climate, we must build upon both Thoreau's commitment to nature —

> *"What is the use of a house if you haven't got a tolerable planet to put it on?"*
> — Letter to Harrison Blake, May 20, 1860

— and his tools of protest.

*"Why does [government] not encourage its citizens to be on
the alert to point out its faults, and do better than it would
have them?"*
— "Civil Disobedience"

In his day, Thoreau wrote, lectured, fought injustice, and lived
life as an individual committed to his principles. So, too, must we
strive to stand up for what we believe is right and just and true as
we struggle with the great challenges of our generation.

Mary Byrne Bergman is a writer and museum director living on Nantucket Island. She is originally from Provincetown.

Old Cape Cod

Mary Byrne Bergman

*"We often love to think now of the life of men on beaches,
at least in midsummer, when the weather is serene; their
sunny lives on the sand, amid the beach-grass and the
bayberries, their companion a cow, their wealth a jag of
driftwood or a few beach-plums, and their music the surf
and the peep of the beach-bird."*
— Henry David Thoreau, *Cape Cod*

Between 1849 and 1855, Henry David Thoreau made four visits
to Cape Cod. The trek from Concord to the spindly spit of sand
was a long one; Thoreau quipped that, "Boston to Provincetown
is twice as far as from England to France." If Henry David were
to venture to the Cape this summer, he'd find himself in bumper-
to-bumper traffic as cars approached the Sagamore Bridge (or
maybe he'd take the Cape Flyer train, the rumble of the rails a
familiar feeling to a man from the 19th century).

On one of his visits, Thoreau scrambled along the backshore
from Eastham to Provincetown, clambering over dunes and
through tidal pools, the scent of beach roses riding on the wind.

"We took to the beach for another day (October 13), walking
along the shore of the resounding sea, determined to get it into
us. We wished to associate with the Ocean until it lost the pond-
like look which it wears to a countryman," he wrote.

The sands have shifted some since Henry David left his footprints
along the coastline, battered by winter storms and four-wheel
drive vehicles. Mercifully, much of the wild sand dune desert
Thoreau wrote of would be familiar to him. In 1961, President

John F. Kennedy (who kept a copy of *Cape Cod* on his bookshelf in Hyannisport) created the Cape Cod National Seashore, preserving 40 miles of Outer Beach.

If Henry David were to make his way down to Provincetown, the sandy fist of the Cape, he would pass T-shirt shops selling salt water taffy and beach plum jam, a jumble of cottage colonies and motor lodges, and little shacks serving fried clams piled high on paper plates. While he might be dismayed at the hordes of tourists that choke the narrow streets of the Cape's towns, he would not be surprised.

Thoreau predicted the Cape's love affair with summer tourism years before it happened:

"The time must come when this coast will be a place of resort for those New-Englanders who really wish to visit the sea-side. At present it is wholly unknown to the fashionable world, and probably it will never be agreeable to them."

Thoreau was there to observe the Cape's inhabitants, but the tables turn when it is Henry David who is under close watch.

"The Cape is so long and narrow, and so bare withal, that it is well-nigh impossible for a stranger to visit it without the knowledge of its inhabitants generally, unless he is wrecked on to it in the night."

Although the Cape's population has grown exponentially since his day, Henry David would still find the same close-knit community among those who dwell at the edge of the world.

I hope that, given Thoreau's attitudes towards civil rights and personal freedom, he would rejoice that Cape Cod has since become a haven for those who live on the fringes of society. Cape Cod is home to fewer fishermen than in Henry David's time, but to more artists, writers, and general rabble-rousers. For many, the Cape is a place to let down your hair and to become your true self.

Deborah Bier is a psychotherapist and internationally respected authority on dementia care, and a 35-year resident of Concord, Massachusetts. A longtime member of the Thoreau Farm Board of Trustees, she is creator of the Thoreau birth house's 1878 kitchen garden.

The Choice of Living Deliberately

Deborah Bier

Have you ever faced your own mortality? I mean, really faced it? Stared unblinkingly down its maw, deep into its bowels? And then looked more? And yet more?

I did once, and it lasted for two years.

It began with a shock followed by a surprise. First, the shock: a totally unexpected diagnosis of a rare and very aggressive cancer. Following a phone call with this news, I roamed around the house in a state of numbness for what might have been a minute, an hour, or half a day. I honestly have no idea — my memory was of trying to stay afloat in a sea of frozen shock.

The surprise followed. Suddenly, Henry Thoreau leaned over and whispered into my ear: "Remember why I went to the woods." This brought me immediately back into the here and now of the world.

I had two simultaneous reactions. First, why was the ghost of Henry Thoreau speaking to me? At the time, I had no devotion to his work or life and was so surprised he had spoken in my ear. The other reaction was that I knew exactly what he meant, even though it had been years since I had read *Walden*.

"I went to the woods because I wished to live deliberately, to front only the essential facts of life, and see if I could not learn what it had to teach, and not, when I came to die, discover that I had not lived," returned to me effortlessly, with nearly perfect recall.

Something about "suck out all the marrow of life…" kept ringing in my ears, though I couldn't capture the rest of the line until I later looked it up in *Walden*.

As I gasped at Henry's words, a review of my life passed before me – how clichéd, I thought, but it was unbidden and out of my control. I saw how I had for a long time lived my life "out loud" and with passion, leading a deliberate existence that in that moment (and many that followed) I felt very proud of. I also understood that no matter how much time I had left, I could continue living deeply, sucking the marrow out of life until the last breath. I knew I could make the process of death as deliberate and open-hearted as I had made living. I felt so deeply and greatly blessed.

Every day of the following two years, I remained in contact with this visit from Henry, keeping it in my mind, allowing it to guide my decisions and activities in work, home, play, friendships, and in my relationships within and with the Concord community where I've lived for 35 years. I relived it during the wee hours of many nights as I wondered when and if there would be the "inevitable" recurrence of the cancer.

I took living deliberately to heart every day. It oddly comforted me to realize that even with a (supposedly) terminal illness, I could die today in an accident. I realized it was best to live every day realizing death could come at any time.

It has been nearly a score of years since my visit from Henry. I have unexpectedly survived without any recurrence of the cancer. Today, in this time of great turmoil in our world, I continue to hold this experience very close inside me where it has become a part of my psychic DNA. I consider it as I ask myself, as many of us do: How shall I protest injustice? Or resist lies and manipulation? Make my own unique contributions to society?

Deliberately, is the answer I always carry with me. I am determined to keep sucking the marrow from life.

Given our changed and changing circumstances, will Henry arrive to again whisper guidance in my ear? Perhaps he will, or perhaps not. It is possible that that one visit from Henry will do. After all, his words from *Walden* will never change ... and that will always be enough.

Photo credit: Molly Eberle

A board member of the Thoreau Farm Trust, Lawrence Buell is Powell M. Cabot Professor of American Literature Emeritus at Harvard University. His books include The Environmental Imagination *(1995),* Writing for an Endangered World *(2001),* Emerson *(2003), and* The Dream of the Great American Novel *(2014). Among other prizes and awards, he has received the John Cawelti Prize for* Writing for an Endangered World *(2002), the Phi Beta Kappa Society's Christian Gauss Award for* Emerson, *and the Modern Language Association's Jay Hubbell Award for lifetime contributions to American Literature studies (2007). His current book-in-progress is on the art and practice of environmental memory.*

What Would Henry Do – About Anything?

Lawrence Buell

How might Thoreau have responded to such burning twenty-first century issues as global warming, widening income inequality, refugee and immigration crises, and insurgent populist nationalism? The challenge of speculating across the centuries on the basis of Thoreau's track record of pronouncements and position-takings on almost every issue is harder than it seems, once you set your mind to it.

On some issues, to be sure, he was pretty consistent, such as nature preservation. On some, he was supportive, but vehement only at intervals, as with abolition. On others, like vegetarianism ("animal food"), he weighed in emphatically now and then, but behaved inconsistently by his own admission. On still others, he more or less mirrored the reformist tune of the time, such as the temperance and labor movements. On still others — immigration, women's rights, and public health reform, for instance — he was a laggard. Thoreau was a ferociously disciplined person who flouted the conventional work ethic to the point that from then to now many have branded him a slacker. His ingenuity enabled his family's pencil-making business to deliver the leading-edge product of its day, yet he railed against the onset of the machine age.

This mixed-bag picture — broadly true for most mortals, but especially conspicuous in a famous figure given to cranky one-liners — makes it impossible to type Thoreau, say, either as a radical progressive or a libertarian, as either pro- *or* anti-

technology. My own preferred approach is to fall back on
Emerson's slightly mind-boggling (but in this case handy)
assertion: "To a sound judgment, the most abstract truth is the
most practical." My answer to the "What would Henry do?"
question, in other words, is to single out a limited number of
Thoreauvian axioms that seem to underlie the mood shifts and
go forward from there. Without pretending to exhaust the list of
possibles, here are three:

1. "It is not a man's duty, as a matter of course, to devote
   himself to the eradication of any, even the most enormous
   wrong . . . but it is his duty, at least, to wash his hands
   of it, and . . . not to give it practically his support" ("Civil
   Disobedience").

   [In other words: my duty to resist a bad status quo begins
   when I sense that it compromises my integrity, and the
   duty is fulfilled more by disengagement than attack.]

2. "The civilized man is a more experienced and wiser
   savage" (*Walden*).

   [In other words, so-called improvements in civilization
   or life-style should be judged in terms of whether they
   enhance or undermine the virtues of "savage" — or
   preindustrial — living.]

3. "Be ever so little distracted . . . that in all places & in all
   hours you can hear the sound of crickets in those seasons
   when they are to be heard. It is a mark of serenity &
   health of mind when a person hears this sound much —
   in streets of cities as well as in fields"
   (*Journal*, 7 July 1851).

   [In other words, humans function best — whether or not
   they happen to be natural historians — in awareness both
   sensory and cognitive of belonging to the surrounding
   biotic world in which mostly invisible life forms call the
   tune to the rhythm of the seasons.]

Start with the likes of these as your postulates, maybe add a couple more, and the chances are that you'll be able to puzzle through more or less to your satisfaction what Henry might have *said or thought* about most, if not all, the burning issues of our day. But when it comes to deciding when and/or whether your revenant Thoreau would have likely have *acted* on those opinions, you're on your own.

Tom Foran Clark was born in southern California and lived
and worked there and in Utah, New Hampshire, France,
and Germany. He has also traveled a good deal in Concord,
Massachusetts. He has worked variously over the years in
advertising as a graphic artist and copy editor, as a quality
assurance controller for assorted eBooks and marketing firms,
and, occasionally, off and on, as a public library director.
Currently he just walks around making notes for books he hopes
yet to write.

Walking Around

Tom Foran Clark

Walking around.

That is what I think Henry would be doing today, just as he did in his time.

Like many of Thoreau's admirers, I first read Thoreau — *Walden,* of course — in my late teens and was startled and awakened by what I found in his writing.

> *"How many a man has dated a new era in his life from the reading of a book?"*

Through more than forty years since — thirty of which I lived in Massachusetts — I have read and contemplated Thoreau's autobiographical and philosophical works, and critical essays galore about his writings, over and over again.

I have discerned, through all that, what I think Thoreau was best at, and what he most liked to do. That was just to walk around looking at things such as they are and, through regarding — just looking at — what has been manifested in the world, discovering what the world is.

It is the present, actual, stumping, glorious "isness" of the world that Thoreau loved.

> *"This was that Earth of which we have heard, made out of Chaos and Old Night. ... Man was not to be associated with it. It was Matter, vast, terrific... rocks, trees, wind on our cheeks! the solid earth! the actual world! the common sense! Contact! Contact!"*

Every Thoreau fan knows how he loved simply to saunter.

When I was a child growing up in California, before I ever read Thoreau's writing, or writings about him, I had encountered a legendary bearded old man named Eiler Larsen, best known as the Laguna Greeter. He was a gardener. He walked around Laguna Beach and often stood, seemingly for days on end, at the then only intersection entering Laguna Beach. He would just wave to people and smile and welcome them.

I think that it was my enjoyment of and fascination with the Laguna Greeter in my early years that made me so receptive and open to Thoreau in my teen years. Not to mention my happy discovery of Walt Whitman: "I loaf and invite my soul, I lean and loaf at my ease observing a spear of summer grass."

As time went on, I found myself most attracted always to writers and writings that echoed this simplicity of just "walking round" looking at things: John Muir, Alan Watts, Jack Kerouac (in his book all about just walking around, *The Dharma Bums*), and Edward Abbey. I've also been fascinated ever since by plenteous stories of such mysterious lone wanderers as Everett Ruess and Chris McCandless.

These were all people who did not want to steer the world, guide the world, lead the world, but rather just to regard the world, and to know the world for just what it is — such as it is — whatever that is.

Thoreau loved solitude, but I could just see him out on a walk with any or all of these other guys and having the time of his life — most especially just afterwards, when he was alone again and could think about it. I think he loved nothing better than the idea of disappearing into the world and becoming wholly part of it.

For me, that is Thoreau in his nutshell: he walked around, regarded the world, thought about it, and wrote out distillations of his findings. That's what I would like people to feel and understand in contemplating "What Thoreau Would Do Now."

Ernesto Estrella completed his Ph.D. at Columbia University in 2007, and between 2007 and 2011 was assistant professor of Contemporary Poetry at Yale University. He is responsible for the most recent and comprehensive Spanish translation of Thoreau's Journal. *In the Spring of 2016, he founded the Nomadic School of the Senses, where he serves as director.*

Carlos Estrella is a journalist, digital communication strategist, cook, and musician, whose work has been developed throughout some of Europe's most prominent media outlets. He serves as Head of Strategy & Communication at the Nomadic School of the Senses.

Henry's LinkedIn Profile (Abridged)

Ernesto Estrella and Carlos Estrella

Bio:

Multifaceted Transcendentalist thinker and innovation manager driven by social impact, environmentalism, and technological progress

Based in the wider Concord, MA, area, I have contributed in many capacities to the development and implementation of sustainable programs at the intersection of Urbanism and Natural Science. As a former educator, I have helped community leaders in the fields of farming, landscaping, and local politics reach high levels of productivity and untapped market opportunities rooted in the understanding of civic responsibility. I believe that a healthy community arises from empowered and mindful individuals. When I hear a customer say they need me for something simple, I encourage them to draft "simple" into a business plan and then come back to me.

Main Featured Skills and Endorsements:

Animal Tracking (10)
Archeology (4)
Water-Measuring (15)
Ornithology (26)
Land-Surveying (22)
Lecturing (5)
Harvesting & Gleaning (17)
Teaching (8)
Creative Writing (17)
Music & Sound Studies (13)
Construction (9)

Selected Recommendations:

Ralph Waldo Emerson (Author and Lecturer)

I have had the pleasure of hiring Mr. H.D. Thoreau's services through the years in different capacities in which he always delivered and, may I add, excelled. I consider myself lucky to be part of his restricted social network of clients and, I would dare say, friends.

Margaret Fuller (Author and Activist)

Great soul, terrible handwriting. He never confessed, but I am sure he used his microscope for his copyediting and proofreading work at The Dial. He was often annoyed by ladies and gentlemen, but loved intensely a few men and women. It looks like he has been opening up a little with time, so let the world enjoy him!

Walt Whitman (Poet)

Thoreau came to visit me on one occasion and was very glad to receive a signed copy of my *Leaves of Grass*. He almost convinced me to add an index at the end of the book specifying the 43 different types of leaf species that can be found in the surroundings of the areas I mention in my book. I finally declined.

John Cage (Composer)

He grew my ears 5mm. He will make your ears grow too. Just listen; just listen.

Gandhi (Political Leader)

The best metaphysical tax-accountant I have ever had. He saw revolution and peace at the bottom of my tea cup. A true community leader.

Bob Dylan (Singer and Noble Prize Winner)

People just don't get him. Need anything, call him. Ask him for a couple of dollars, and he will give them away. But do not steal his afternoons from him.

Richard Branson (CEO, Virgin)

I have heard he walks like Indian hunters did. Do you need anything else for a premium entrepreneur?

Michelle Obama (Former First Lady and Activist)

Had Barack only known a couple of years ago that he was available! He took the "fired up" a little too literally on a couple of occasions, but, boy, was he ready to go! I hear "Thoreau" and I think "successful children's education."

John Legere (CEO, T-Mobile)

Age and over-qualification have never been an issue when it comes to hiring new talent. Read his paragraphs on the telegraph: Thoreau is Connectivity before Connectivity!

Alicia Keys (Singer/Songwriter)

Hang a picture of this wild man by your mirror, forget about the make-up, record a great album, and go for a walk. Thanks, Henry David!

Languages

English, French, German, Latin, Greek (Advanced/Native level)

Italian, Spanish, Sanskrit, Mandarin, Hebrew (Reading proficiency)

Michael J. Frederick is the executive director of The Thoreau Society, Inc.

Golden Compass

Michael J. Frederick

It tasks the imagination to conceive of how Henry might respond to particular contemporary issues, especially in determining what he might actually do in any given situation. He is a fairly nimble specimen to pin down. But through his published writings, we have inherited an extensive record of his ideals, many of which were cultivated by him in the verdant fields of New England Transcendentalist thought during the 19th century.

Henry's actual time and place is forever in the past. The conditions, both inner and outer, that produced and sustained him throughout his lifetime are no more. But Henry's wisdom, we have heard it said, is perennial, timeless, and eternal. Like the hound, the bay horse, and the turtledove, we are still on its trail. So let us invoke imagination. With a little intention of the eye, let us envision Henry taking root in 2017, surrounded by our own technocratic, consumer-driven society.

We send a distinguished naturalist to observe transplanted Henry. As it turns out, this particular variety of Henry has continuity from one generation to the next in at least one important characteristic. He strives for authenticity and self-actualization in the highest sense. He lives a considered and deliberate life, desiring to live a fully human life under any conditions, practicing the art of self-cultivation. He wears two watches, one on his wrist for time and another in his pocket, affixed to his jacket by a golden chain, for eternity.

Our next discovery will probably surprise those readers who are somewhat acquainted with Henry's actual history; it will certainly astound those of you who know nothing about it. We discovered

Henry living alone, in the woods, in close proximity to neighbors, in a house which he had built himself, on the shore of White Pond, in Concord, Massachusetts, on privately owned land.

Walden Pond today is owned and managed by the Commonwealth of Massachusetts for the benefit of the public, which Henry is quite happy about, stating that it is the first step toward us having "instead of noblemen … noble villages of men." But because he could not secure the requisite building permits from the state, he decided to build his solar-powered cabin instead at Walden's "sister" pond, White Pond. The two ponds are not, as many still believe, connected to one another by underground currents, although the belief persists — though they know not why — because an unconscious current, only hinted at, runs through and connects all times, places, and things.

Henry spends his mornings at the pond writing a book on what he is calling the "perennial philosophy," a term borrowed from Aldous Huxley, who is more familiarly known for his *Brave New World* than his writings on wisdom literature. I would explain more, but I have no time for that.

In writing his book, *On Golden Pond,* or *White Pond during the Golden Hour*, Henry is considering a variety of approaches to life and the conundrums that are inextricably woven into the fabric of living in the world ethically. Hinduism and Buddhism figure in prominently for their abstract philosophy. Apparently, Henry sometimes feels himself to be a Self with a capital "S," or Atman, as the *Bhagavad Gita* and the *Upanishads* teach. Our naturalist is a bit confused by a seeming contradiction in Henry's writing, for as he celebrates the eternal Self in one place, in another he writes to a friend to say, "I am nothing." So far, we believe this is not a statement of low self-esteem, but possibly a Buddhistic insight, regarding "no-self."

While many of Thoreau's neighbors are leading lives of quiet desperation and have to console themselves in their rural backyards with the bravery of minks and muskrats, Henry is able to meet monthly expenses mainly through the labor of his hands, with the exception that he occasionally contributes blog posts for the ACLU and 350.org on social and environmental issues. He devotes about 10 hours a week to labor and has the rest free for study and the perception of goodness, truth, and beauty.

He says: "One attraction in coming to the woods to live was that I should have leisure and opportunity to see the spring come in."

In the social arena, we have learned that Henry views his move to White Pond as a form of resistance to prevailing societal norms and an economy based on fossil fuels. Speaking at Thoreau Farm recently, Henry advised audiences, in the vein of Socrates, to "know thy self." Then he continued, "Let your life be a counter friction to stop the machine."

Jayne Gordon is the former Director of Education and Public Programs at the Massachusetts Historical Society, and the former Executive Director of the Thoreau Society. A resident of Concord, she regularly teaches and lectures about aspects of the town's history, drawing on her experience working as a staff or board member, consultant, or partner with almost all of Concord's historical organizations over the past 45 years. Currently, she is on the boards of the Robbins House and the Friends of Minute Man National Park, and she will be the project director for the Concord Museum's two summer teacher workshops on Thoreau in 2017, to be offered at Thoreau Farm and funded by the National Endowment for the Humanities.

What Would Henry Thoreau Do When Confronted with Modern–Day Political, Environmental, or Social Issues?

Jayne Gordon

He would ask questions. Hard, penetrating, uncomfortable questions. Questions that are as thought provoking in our time as they were in his. Questions that informed Thoreau's actions. They can inspire our own.

I try to avoid guessing how Thoreau would react to specific challenges that we face today. I can't get inside his head. He's dead, and not commenting on our dilemmas at present. But I can look at how he approached the issues of his own time. I can identify and investigate the timeless questions he raised. And then I can apply those questions to the considerations and choices before us today as we try to live with integrity in this messy, complex, complicated, conflicted world. That's not so easy right now!

Here are some of Thoreau's questions that I have found to be most helpful. They don't lead to easy answers. They are disturbing. They are maddening. But they force us to confront how we might live our lives as principled, thoughtful members of both social and natural communities, and as individuals with intact, hard-working consciences.

These questions range through the personal, philosophical, and political arenas. For Thoreau, I believe those were inseparable.

From "Civil Disobedience":

"How does it become a man to behave toward this American government today?"

"Must the citizen ever for a moment, or in the least degree, resign his conscience to the legislator? Why has every man a conscience, then?"

"How can a man be satisfied to entertain an opinion merely, and enjoy it?"

From "Slavery in Massachusetts":

"Who can be serene in a country where both the rulers and the ruled are without principle?"

From "A Plea for Captain John Brown":

"Is it not possible that an individual may be right and a government wrong? Are laws to be enforced simply because they are made and declared by any number of men to be good, if they are not good? Is there any necessity for a man's being a tool to perform a deed of which his better nature disapproves?"

"What right have you to enter into a compact with yourself that you will do thus and so, against the light within you?"

From "Life Without Principle":

"Do we call this the land of the free? What is it to be free from King George and continue the slaves of King Prejudice? What is it to be born free and not to live free? What is the value of political freedom, but as a means to moral freedom?"

From "Walking":

"What business have I in the woods, if I am thinking of something out of the woods?"

From *Walden*:

"Could a greater miracle take place than for us to look through each other's eyes for an instant?" — "Economy"

"Why should we live with such hurry and waste of life?" — "Where I Lived and What I Lived For"

"What is a course of history or philosophy, or poetry, no matter how well selected, or the best society, or the most admirable routine of life, compared with the discipline of looking always at what is to be seen?" — "Sounds"

"How can you expect the birds to sing when their groves are cut down?" — "The Ponds"

"Why should we be in such desperate haste to succeed and in such desperate enterprises?" — "Conclusion"

From Thoreau's letters and journals:

"What is the use of a house if you haven't got a tolerable planet to put it on?"

"A man may acquire a taste for wine or brandy, and so lose his love for water, but should we not pity him?"

"A man must generally get away some hundreds or thousands of miles from home before he can be said to begin his travels. Why not begin his travels at home? Would he have to go very far or look very closely to discover new novelties?"

"It is not enough to be industrious; so are the ants. What are you industrious about?"

Tim Hebert currently serves as Chief Client Officer of Carousel Industries in Rhode Island and is working on a book called Unguarded Moments, *a business leadership book with a Transcendentalism theme.*

We Can Have the Courage

Tim Hebert

One winter morning long ago, I sat daydreaming in my American Literature high school class. I was a mediocre student at best, but my teacher would often tell my parents otherwise and lament about my wasted potential. Many of us have been the subject of one of those dreaded parent-teacher conferences.

That morning, I was staring out the window when Mrs. Harden noticed I was not paying attention and so, of course, called upon me to read aloud a passage from an essay the class was studying: "Self-Reliance", by Ralph Waldo Emerson.

As the laughter in the room rose, everyone assuming I would at best muddle the passage though more likely totally embarrass myself, I struggled to find my place in the text, then read in a quivering voice: "Trust thyself: every heart vibrates to that iron string."

My voice broke as I read that final word — "string." I proceeded to reread the line to the class again, and then again and again. I just could not get past it to the next line. I was stuck in a loop.

Something about that sentence had struck a chord with me, playing through my mind relentlessly even as I walked down to the principal's office. "Trust thyself," I kept hearing, "every heart vibrates to that iron string."

I skipped the next seven days of school and began devouring everything I could get my hands on written by Emerson and Thoreau. I came across an equally formidable sentence by Thoreau in one of his journals: "The price of anything is the amount of life you exchange for it." Once again, a sentence on a page written long ago rang out to me like a big bell, then refused to settle down and leave my mind alone.

The words of these two 19th century thinkers spoke directly to me, comforting me in a time of personal confusion. They leaped off the page and raced my way, affecting me and altering me. I had suddenly acquired (and still possess) a voracious appetite for Emerson, Thoreau, and the rest of the Transcendentalists. Their words delivered to me three curious details that would shape the man I would become: the importance of learning, the power of choice, and the courage of Integrity.

Almost fifty years later, I now, again, often sit quietly staring out my window, daydreaming and wondering about these uncertain times. I'm concerned about the fate of our country and troubled by our newfound casual lack of humanity. In this particular unguarded moment, a question forms: "What would Henry and Ralph Waldo do?" Would they sit still with quieted voices in the shadows? Or would they vigorously preach atop a soapbox? Or would they stand up in defiance?

Unfortunately, I can't speak for those great men, but I can employ my own voice and actions, as can all of us. So therefore what can *I* do? More importantly, what can *we* do?

I have come up with some answers:

We can seek the truth! We can swim through an ocean of falsehoods, knowledge, and past wisdom to illuminate new ideas and thoughts. We can learn to discern between "fake news" and propaganda and political rhetoric, to discover obvious or hidden genuine kernels of truth. We have an opportunity to turn our country into something remarkable, though we cannot accomplish this only with what we know today. It will require us to welcome new thoughts, experience new ideas, and shed light on new knowledge.

We can also understand the power of choice. We can choose how we respond to the world around us. Do we sit by and let someone else do something? Or do we each take some kind of action — large or small — and become the change ourselves?

Finally, we can have the courage of integrity. Like Thoreau and Emerson, we can grab onto the courage to truly know who we are, what we stand for, and what we are willing to fight for. We can have the courage to be authentic in the tempest, choosing to extend succor over building walls, seek truth over the spreading of falsehoods, or opt for sacrifice over convenience.

I will close with one final Thoreau quote: "A single footstep will not make a path on the earth."

We have the chance to blaze a meaningful trail through these uncertain times. But merely a single action, an individual thought, or an isolated experience will not leave a trace. To make the deepest impression, we must faithfully follow the paths we create over and over and over again.

So ask yourself, where are you today? What must you do?

Then bravely walk on, stepping forward on your chosen path, and leave your mark.

Ronald Wesley Hoag is a professor of English at East Carolina University in Greenville, North Carolina, a member of the Thoreau Society board of directors, and a past editor of The Concord Saunterer: A Journal of Thoreau Studies. *A former Needham, Massachusetts, boy, Hoag fished in Walden Pond before he knew who Henry Thoreau was.*

The Whole Circle of Experience

Ronald Wesley Hoag

AUTHOR'S NOTE: I'll start by playing devil's advocate, then play "What If?" Since HDT is in fact dead (last summer I saw the hearse that carried him to at least one of his two graves), propositions based on "if he were alive today" are hypotheses contrary to fact, a classic logical fallacy.

But another fact we cannot deny is that times change and time changes. Several people I know — and some I don't — have been referred to in print as Thoreau channelers. All of them are good Thoreauvians and Thoreau scholars. None of them is Henry Thoreau. Even quoting Thoreau's own stated opinions is tricky, not just because the world — and world views — differ now, but because he himself changed his mind: over his lifetime, from day to day, from minute to minute, and for the most part deliberately. Henry's ideas were his daily weather, and he was a New Englander, after all. Therefore, like the Bible, Thoreau can be accurately quoted, but also misrepresented, by taking him out of context.

Further complicating the problem, some of what is attributed to him he never said at all, like my seafood restaurant T-shirt proclaiming, "Everyone must believe something. I believe I will go fishing. — Thoreau." Clever enough, but also apocryphal.

Since Thoreau was, as one of his poems declares, a centaur, with a physical body and a roving mind and spirit, he speaks variously from different positions along a dualistic continuum, ranging from "driftwood in the stream" to "Indra in the sky looking down on it" (*Walden*). He claims the freedom to be, by turns, all-in physically, all-in spiritually, and sometimes in-the-all all-at-once.

He wants the whole circle of experience, not by forsaking earth for heaven but by finding heaven under his feet as well as over his head. He is true to the moment that moves him, inconsistent and contradictory, but deliberately so.

Emerson says that "a foolish consistency is the hobgoblin of little minds," and that "with consistency a great soul has simply nothing to do." That was Henry, a great soul in precept and practice.

Walden's "Brute Neighbors" chapter follows "Higher Laws," a chapter that opens with the temptation to devour a live woodchuck and then moves to a vegan-like rejection of animal food. Yet in "Brute Neighbors," the Thoreauvian hermit must answer an immediate question: "The world lay about at this angle"— namely, "Shall I go to heaven or a-fishing?" When the hermit leaves his hollow tree to take up his fishing pole, Thoreau shows that pursuing transcendence does not require leaving flesh and blood behind. Re-creation may be found in recreation as well as in contemplation. "There never is but one opportunity of a kind," says the hermit, while demonstrating that the way to improve any opportunity is through immersion in its experience. So concludes the hermit—and his chapter.

Logical fallacies aside, I'll take this opportunity to play "What would Henry do (or think or say) if he were here today?" The economics-driven, scale-tipping role of civilization in climate change would likely not shock the man who both chronicled seasonal growth and observed that most people literally and figuratively sell nature short. And while the Maine woods would still beckon Thoreau, its forested riverside beauty strips masking logged-out interiors would make him curse the unkind cut, just as he once mourned a logger-felled pine, gone, he fancied, to as high a heaven as he would go to, there to tower above him still.

On the plus side, he would, I think, be gratified by today's chorus of support for his assertion that wildness preserves the world, and he would take heart from our actually having preserved parts of the Maine woods and other wilderness areas, as prescribed in his essay "Chesuncook." (He might, though, question the oxymoronic notion of a managed wilderness and be wary of visitor invasions.) As for sublime and sacred Katahdin, his holy mountain, he would elevate Percival Baxter's gift to the people of Maine but prick the inflated hubris implicit in giving a mountain away.

Finally, if Henry Thoreau were alive today, he would echo his letter to H.G.O. Blake, in which he linked his own pondered experiences to the meaning inherent in nature: "The *truth* is still *true*," he wrote. "Katahdin is there still"— and so is "my old conviction." I'd like to think he would do such things.

Shoko Itoh, Ph.D., is Professor Emeritus at Hiroshima University and the past president of Japan Thoreau Society. She is a translator of Faith in a Seed *and* Wild Fruits. *She has published four books, including* Dismal Swamp *and* American Renaissance.

Two Major Ideological Frameworks of "Civil Disobedience:" The Philosophy of Neighbor and Ecological Thought

Shoko Itoh

"Civil Disobedience" has two significant ideological frameworks: the Philosophy of Neighbor and Ecological Thought.

First, "Civil Disobedience" calls for the novel Philosophy of Neighbor in modern America. In American society, Thoreau's contemporaries had been supported by "manifest destiny," based on the political idea that selected people (white Americans) would settle the western frontier.

On the night of July 24, 1846, Thoreau viewed the town of Concord from his jail window. The town was separated from him by the jail wall, and as an outsider in a State institution, he realized the essence of the Concord community. To them, a neighbor was a neighbor within the community they belonged to: a Concord resident or an American. Thoreau refers to "his neighbor, your neighbor." Thoreau's distinctive use of the words "our neighbor," or simply "neighbors," however, meant a neighbor of any kind living anywhere, including minorities such as immigrant Americans, black and Native Americans, and even Mexican people, who were now in the country because of American invasion.

As discussed in my book, *Yomigaeru Soro (Sauntering to the Inner Wilderness)*, the use of the word "neighbor(s)" — repeated twenty times in the text — pursued the concept of neighbor espoused in the "Parable of the Good Samaritan," a didactic story told by Jesus and depicted exclusively in Luke. In this respect, it would be no exaggeration to say that "Civil Disobedience" was indeed an article about neighbors.

Thoreau's concept of neighbor further appeared in the magnified form of "world citizen" in the "Sounds" chapter of *Walden*. The "world citizen" therein is an indication of the epiphany that the emergence of global consumers, owing to the distribution of goods made possible by the railways, could alter the quality of citizens from being restricted to one town or one nation to belonging to a class of economic "world citizens," wherein people would profit from obtaining products, as commercial goods, from the back yard of the globe. Thoreau's cross-regional ethical norm was further related in "Civil Disobedience," and in fact, is found in the final section:

> *"I please myself with imagining a State at least which can afford to be just to all men, and to treat the individual with respect as a neighbor; which even would not think it inconsistent with its own repose, if a few were to live aloof from it, not meddling with it, nor embraced by it, who fulfilled all the duties of neighbors and fellow-men. A State which bore this kind of fruit, and suffered it to drop off as fast as it ripened, would prepare the way for a still more perfect and glorious State, which also I have imagined, but not yet anywhere seen."*

Shown here is the second ideological framework, which is an ecological idea or an idea that nature and society are fundamentally unified, by comparing justice to a seed that will bear fruit without fail.

Thoreau once again repeats the word "neighbor(s)" without pronouns and ends with a botanical statement: "A State which bore this kind of fruit, and suffered it to drop off as fast as it ripened, would prepare the way for a still more perfect and glorious State."

This is a sincere conclusion corresponding to a great faith in a seed, as is seen in the manuscript, *Faith in a Seed*. A seed is, for Thoreau, a good beginning and, as such, faith in the seed overlaps with his expectation that the construction of a State composed of such neighbors will be accomplished.

In addition, "If a plant cannot live according to its nature, it dies; and so a man" indicates an ecological view of a fundamentally unified society and nature.

This idea, which is extremely characteristic of Thoreau, is also expressed in "The Succession of Forest Trees," an essay on natural history that forms part of *Faith in a Seed*, as follows:

> *"Convince me that you have a seed there, and I am prepared to expect wonders. I shall even believe that the millennium is at hand, and that the reign of justice is about to commence, when the Patent Office, or Government, begins to distribute, and the people to plant, the seeds of these things."*

The idea of the government as the Patent Office for seed distribution depicts the government as being set within the mechanism and not as the machine itself. Accordingly, for Thoreau, neighbors encompass nature, human beings, and all of society, including wild creatures.

This is a revision of a section from Chapter 8 of Shoko Itoh's book in Japanese from NHK publication, Thoreau for Beginners, A Message from the Woods, *(Dec. 2016), pp. 90-93.*

Maria Madison is the President/Cofounder of The Robbins House Board. Her career has blended community work with international health and clinical research. Currently she is a Fulbright Specialist as well as Adjunct Faculty with the University of Global Health Equity in Kigali, Rwanda (Partners in Health). She is a longtime Concord resident and married to a pretty extraordinary spouse with two exceptionally wonderful young adults.

Documenting What Others Do Not See

Maria Madison

"It's not what you look at that matters. It's what you see."

Henry David Thoreau is credited with making this statement. He spent countless hours looking, seeing, reflecting upon, and writing about living simply in the natural surroundings of Walden Pond and Concord, Massachusetts. He wrote at length about nature's details, aspects of the world others looked at daily but failed to see. Thoreau's goal seemed to be to document the essence of nature and what it means to be alive.

On February 2, 1859, Thoreau wrote, "I see Peter Hutchinson cutting down a large red oak on A. Heywood's hillside. He points out to me what he calls the 'gray oak' there with 'a thicker bark' than the red. It is the scarlet oak."

Two remarkable things happen here. First, Peter Hutchinson isn't just looking at trees; he "sees" the trees, and the two men confer about the red, gray, and scarlet oak trees. Second, Thoreau documents the conversation in his journal. By all accounts this sounds like a conversation between equals about nature, though one man is black, one is white, and it's the mid-19th century. The exchange was remarkable enough to be etched in one of the most timeless journals ever written. Contrary to Ralph Ellison's symbolic *Invisible Man*, written in 1952, Thoreau "saw" Peter in 1859.

Thoreau saw what others looked past. So what would Thoreau do with a cell phone?

The Internet is replete with comments of how Thoreau would eschew cell phones as a major distraction to nature and society:

"Thoreau would be pissed off because of the lack of simplicity," "Thoreau would say technology pulls us away from our natural environment," and "Thoreau would describe how though a person can travel by train and get to his or her destination quicker, the life experience that she or he is missing out on is more important than the time it took to get there."

There could have been greater simplicity had Colson Whitehead's *Underground Railroad* truly existed alongside the cell phone in the 19th century. I believe Thoreau would pick up a cell phone without hesitation and call a stationmaster on the Underground Railroad. I believe he would catalog infinite new species of plants and consult the world's geographers, naturalists, explorers, philosophers, and scientists. Ring ... ring ... calling all cosmologists.

If someone dialed Thoreau, he would surely answer the call ... to make his case on behalf of nature and toward a more civil society. With the tap of a button, Thoreau could instantly catalog humanity's diversity. By pressing a key, Thoreau would use the cell phone to negotiate the social contract, expediting social change with his fingertips!

On October 1, 1851, Thoreau documented helping to transport a "fugitive slave," who had taken the name of Henry Williams, to safety in Canada. A cell phone in Thoreau's hands, and in the hands of all of the other antislavery activists before him, could have advanced the antislavery movement in immeasurable ways.

Thoreau's hunger for detail would have compelled him to photograph Henry Williams' face. What might Henry Williams' face have told us that Thoreau could not capture in a journal entry? Thoreau's journal entry refers to Williams as "well behaved," though a photo might have shown a full-grown, upright man – beaten down by circumstance. The cell phone photo might have screamed, "this is a man terrorized by his environment" as opposed to "well behaved." Thoreau would have appreciated the dialogue such a photo would have inspired among his fellow Transcendentalists. The cell phone photo might have helped Thoreau depict the genocidal act that was slavery.

When debating what Thoreau would do in modern times, we are reminded that Thoreau put nature first, and, despite his saying "men have become the tools of their tools," would have greatly appreciated the lightning speed with which the cell phone would have helped to document truth and move science, humanity, and civil societies forward.

Thoreau, bound by conscience and a good heart, would have appreciated both the infinite ability to document the vastness of nature through photographs and the rapidity of sounding the alarm of injustice.

If Thoreau showed any hesitation at all, I would tell him to pick up the d@#$@$n phone!

Photo credit: Andy Newman

Gregory Maguire has lived in Concord since late 1994. He is a novelist for adults and children; his best-known book is Wicked, *which inspired the Broadway musical of the same name. A popular speaker here and abroad, Gregory Maguire has also spent his career in advocacy work for children and reading.*

Time Travel in Concord

Gregory Maguire

It seems to me that, for those of us who have already grown up, a children's book can be a kind of time machine. If we have read it in childhood and loved it well enough to reread it, we are returned nose-to-page in contact with a more magical, puzzling universe — one perhaps more filled with possibilities than we have come, now, to believe in. It's a kind of time travel, returning to us something lost. (Ask Proust about this.)

"How many a man has dated a new era in his life from the reading of a book," wrote Thoreau in his essay, "Reading." I suggest there are few Western children who haven't inaugurated a new era from reading.

One of the reasons I moved to Concord was because of books I loved in childhood. Jane Langton set in Concord her seven children's fantasies, published from 1962 through 2008. Suffused with a summer-grass bouquet of homegrown Transcendentalism, these books follow the quixotic adventures of a lumpy family —we might now call it blended — who live in Concord, on the south side of Walden Street. (The house is still there; it's that late Victorian villa with the magnificent turret. Just across from Heywood Meadow.)

Starting with *The Diamond in the Window*, Ms. Langton slyly slips scraps of wisdom from Emerson and Thoreau and Oliver Wendell Holmes into her novels, like cryptic messages threaded into fortune cookies from Chang An, a local restaurant. A favorite character, eccentric Concordian Uncle Freddy, makes samplers in lazy-daisy stitch for his young charges. "Fish in the sky! H. D. T." and "Hitch your wagon to a star! R. W. E." These aren't just bumper stickers for a ride into the ethereal; the notions predict and govern the enchanted dream adventure that the children of the house will experience in the next few pages.

In the fifth book in the series, *The Time Bike*, young Eddy receives the present of a new bike. It comes all the way from India. Like other presents in other books, this bike has a mystical quality. It's equipped with a dial that allows it to wheel backward and forward in time.

When Eddy's aunt writes Henry David Thoreau's name and a date on a blackboard — 1817 — Eddy doesn't wait to notice that she will continue writing — "Henry David Thoreau, 1817-1862." He rushes away and sets his bike to plunge back in time to early nineteenth century Concord. Now he has the chance to meet one of his family heroes.

He expects to arrive at Walden Pond, but overshoots.

"There was no pond in sight, nor any small house in the woods. But there was a bigger house of rough, unpainted boards, turned silvery gray by the sun. Chickens stepped daintily here and there in the yard, pecking at the dirt. . .

"It was a farm, a real old Concord farm. Back in this early time most of the town had been farms like this, not real estate developments with split-level houses and asphalt driveways and swimming pools. Henry was probably out there in the field, plowing or feeding the pigs."

The joke isn't drawn out for too long. He sees a woman milking a cow, "a healthy-looking woman wearing an apron over a long, drab dress. Her hair was tucked into a cap tied under her chin....

" '...Isn't this where Henry lives?' said Eddy. 'Henry Thoreau?'

" 'Henry Thoreau! There's no Henry here... unless you mean David Henry Thoreau?'... The woman disappeared into the house... A moment later she came back, holding a baby. 'Here he is, boy. This is David Henry Thoreau. He's ten days old.'

"Eddy gaped at the baby. He didn't know what to say. 'Well, he sure is cute,' he mumbled at last. But the baby wasn't cute. David Henry's little face was purple, he was whimpering and squirming, and he was ugly as sin." (*The Time Bike*, 91-93)

I laughed again while rereading this chapter on the two-hundredth anniversary of Thoreau's birth. He comes alive for me as an ugly infant just as he comes alive for me in the pages of his own magnificent writing. An ugly baby is a wild thing, as close to nature at the age of ten days as any other moment of Thoreau's wild and civilized life. "In wildness is the preservation of the world," he wrote. Thoreau's great quote is the epigraph for the most luminous of Jane Langton's novels, *The Fledgling*. She reminds us that H.D.T. is talking also about the wildness of children.

A wildness to which we do well to return, as often as we can — if not in the pages of a book, then on the pages of the world in which wildness is preserved. Our childhood reading returns us to ourselves. Refreshed, we carry on.

Photo credit: Molly Eberle

Jack Maguire is David's father, a citizen of Concord, and a member of Thoreau Farm's Board of Trustees.

A Celebration: Two Concord Davids Stand Alone

Jack Maguire

Historic Concord has been my family's hallowed home for almost forty years. My two heroes named David were both born here in Concord. The following poem, *The Creation of David*, is dedicated to my son David Maguire and to his namesake, David Henry Thoreau:

The Creation of David

A quirky quantum trace
Froths from its timeless sea,
Inflating, creating space.
The Cosmos is free!

Waves of radiation flash
Across the swelling sphere,
As energetic photons clash,
And massive quarks appear.

When protons and electrons form
As ions in a plasma ball,
Neutrinos penetrate and swarm
And cooling atoms finally fall.

At once the universe expands
And gravity becomes the force
To execute Einstein's commands —
The stellar and galactic source.

In time the supernovas fuse
Carbon, iron, stuff of life,
Until more cataclysms choose
Planets, moons and Darwin's strife.

Our Earth is only one blue dot
A haven in this cosmic storm
Where once the dinosaurs were taught
That here a firestorm could form.

Are Egypt's pharaohs still in power?
Did Ozymandias survive?
Have tyrants thwarted freedom's flower?
Can truth and love and beauty thrive?

Ten billion years have now gone by;
Man muses on his early throne,
Reflecting on the wondrous sky —
While loving David stands alone.

David Maguire was born with cerebral palsy and language disabilities. His parents were told by his doctors that he would likely never walk, talk, or attend regular schools. But David's indomitable spirit resulted in the miracle of a four-year college degree and the character of one of the finest, kindest young men I have ever known.

It should be clear in interpreting this humble poem that David's proud dad is more a scientist than a poet. The poem traces a Scientist/Transcendentalist's view of how our universe, planet, and mankind evolved from the Big Bang to our precarious present state as we celebrate Thoreau's 200th birthday.

Here is where David Henry Thoreau (only after graduating from Harvard in his 20s did Thoreau arbitrarily transpose his name to Henry David) enters the poem's picture:

- **Thoreau the Scientist** was one of the earliest strong supporters of "Darwin's strife," the theory of evolution. Thoreau had read with enthusiasm Charles Darwin's *On the Origin of Species* and challenged other prominent scholars of his day who doubted evolution. Today Thoreau would be in the forefront of those endorsing natural selection as a fundamental principle of science.

- **Thoreau the Naturalist** would have continued to be our champion of conservation. He studied the subtle changes over time in the habitats of flora and fauna at Walden Pond, in Walden Woods, and all along the Concord River. Henry would have been a dedicated defender of Planet Earth — Carl Sagan's Pale Blue Dot — against the ravages of over-industrialization and human-induced global warming.

- **Thoreau the Freedom-Fighting Pacifist**, memorialized on the Great Stone Circle in Walden Woods by Mohandas Gandhi, Emily Dickinson, and Martin Luther King, would today still be an advocate of Percy B. Shelley's stand against tyranny and slavery in his powerful sonnet, *Ozymandias*.

    "... Nothing beside remains. Round the decay
    Of that colossal Wreck, boundless and bare
    The lone and level sands stretch far away."

Henry would have responded passionately to two of the poem's questions, especially foreboding today: Did Ozymandias survive? And have tyrants thwarted freedom's flower?

- **Thoreau the Transcendentalist**, philosopher — lover of wisdom — partnered with fellow Concordians Emerson, the Alcotts, Margaret Fuller, and Hawthorne — among our greatest Americans — in affirmatively answering the poem's profound question, "Can truth and love and beauty thrive?"

The primary inspiration of "The Creation of David" has been my son David. Thoreau's fellow Concordian exemplifies David Henry's ideals in the heroic, yet humble way he lives his life of challenges.

David cherishes the wisdom of Dr. Seuss's Lorax, also carved in stone in Walden Woods: "Unless someone like you cares a whole awful lot, nothing's going to get better; it's not."

Hence a most fitting ending to *The Creation of David*: "Loving David stands alone."

Peter Manso's Ptown: Art, Sex and Money on the Outer Cape *was a triple book-club selection and* Boston Globe *No. 1 bestseller. Both his Norman Mailer and Marlon Brando biographies were nominated for the Pulitzer Prize.*

Return to Cape Cod

Peter Manso

In this frightening era of Trump, perhaps the best thing for me to do would be to forsake Berkeley and return to my house on Long Nook Road [in Truro, Massachusetts], and like Henry David Thoreau, stand on the high cliff overlooking the beach and "put all of America behind me."

Photo credit: BayColonyMedia.com/Christopher Brown

Kristi Lynn Martin is a doctoral candidate in American and New England Studies, Boston University. A Transcendentalist at heart, she has studied Concord, Massachusetts' literary circle for more than twenty years and enjoys reading and spending time outdoors, especially with her cat, Bob. Originally from Rochester, New York, Kristi now lives and works in Concord as a museum professional and historical interpreter at Thoreau Farm.

The "Problem" of Thoreau: Challenging the Reader to Inspire the Reader

Kristi Lynn Martin

What would Henry do?

When posed with the question of what a historical figure would do in a particular situation, in a time in which that individual did not live, one can only speculate. At best, inspiration can be found in the past for our own actions in the present. Henry David Thoreau played with the concept of time and the individual's place within historical memory.

In *A Week on the Concord and Merrimack Rivers,* he wrote that when truth was extracted from chronology, the dates would be shed "like withered leaves," and history would be rendered timeless, like truth itself.

Allowing for, in Thoreauvian fashion, informed observation and imaginative fancy to lead toward the transcendent truth of the inquiry, this essay addresses the challenges that Thoreau directly puts to his readers. And the question "What would Henry do?" presents the particular "problem" of looking to Thoreau for guidance.

Recent debates over the relevance of Thoreau remind us that readers' responses to his writings differ widely while the conversation's very existence reasserts the author's relevance. One's relationship with Thoreau can change with each reading. If this line of reflection is not wholly original, it is timely, and perhaps this essay will have something original, or at least inspiring, to say on the topic.

Thoreau took hard moral stands that can be alienating in their tone. Whether he's charging his readers to resist unjust laws, in "Resistance to Civil Government" and his other abolitionist writings, or criticizing their lifestyle in *Walden*, Thoreau's principles can be acerbic and condemning. He intended to be provocative, to wake his readers up to principled consciousness. The demands Thoreau makes on readers can seem antithetical to modern life. This aspect of Thoreau's writing may give the impression that the author is unsympathetic to his reader, who may feel morally judged, and reject Thoreau before arriving at the author's greater point. This might be especially true for those readers who are introduced to Thoreau in a classroom, through the limited scope of "Economy," the first chapter of *Walden*.

In "Economy," Thoreau describes his reader's "mean and sneaking lives," "stealing time" from their creditors to read his book. He lectures against the trumpery of unnecessary material belongings that become a burden, and asks his readers to reconsider their lifestyles. Thoreau particularly addressed "Economy" to poor students.

A Harvard graduate, Thoreau wrote in *Walden* that students "should not play life, or study it merely, while the community supports them at the expensive game, but earnestly live it from beginning to end."

If a modern reader is perchance a student taking on exorbitant debt for an education, enjoys the pleasure of new clothing, or doesn't aspire to live in a tiny house, is that individual failing as a reader of Thoreau? Or failing to be properly "Thoreauvian?"

These same sticking points in Thoreau's rhetoric have led to his being reduced and labeled by readers who are either affronted or flattered by quotes lifted out of his texts. There is the myth of the hermit, the hypocrite, the naturalist, the mystic, and the civil liberties hero to be contended with. One must also differentiate between Thoreau the narrative persona, Thoreau the writer, and Thoreau the person. There are layers of context that mediate all of these understandings.

Thoreau could be a difficult person, but also an extraordinarily inspiring one. He wanted to provoke his readers to live more consciously, with deliberate awareness, rather than to follow any particular action he advocated.

Concluding "Economy," he wrote, "I would not have any one adopt my mode of living on any account; for besides that before he has fairly learned it I may have found out another for myself, I desire that there may be as many different persons in the world as possible; but I would have each one be very careful to find out and pursue *his own way*, and not his father's or mother's or his neighbors' instead."

The question Thoreau puts to his readers is, rather, do you live deliberately?

Filmmaker/writer Ivy Meeropol is best known for her 2004 film,
Heir to An Execution, *about the legacy of her grandparents, Julius
and Ethel Rosenberg (Sundance Film Festival, Academy Award
short-list, HBO). Her film* Indian Point *questions safety standards
overseen by the U.S. Nuclear Regulatory Commission in light
of Japan's Fukushima Daiichi disaster – while observing daily
operations at an aging nuclear power plant just 35 miles north of
New York City (Winner of MacArthur Foundation documentary
grant, premiere at 2015 Tribeca Film Festival). Meeropol created
and directed the nonfiction television series,* The Hill *(Sundance
Channel), a comedic, behind-the-scenes look at the young
staffers of a US Congressman (2007 International Documentary
Association nominee for Best Limited Series). Meeropol was senior
producer of CNN Films'* The End: Inside the Last Days of the
Obama White House. *She is also a director for CNN's* Death Row
Stories *and National Geographic's* Years of Living Dangerously.

A Peaceful Spot in the Woods

Ivy Meeropol

I think the first thing Thoreau would do if he were with us today is take a long walk in a peaceful wood. At least that's how I imagine it.

He would not, as I did when faced with the awful truth that Donald J. Trump had won the Presidency, drink himself sick on wine and then huddle under the covers for a couple of days. I did just that; pulling the shades, leaving the kids and husband to fend for themselves, while I experienced real grief and physical pain, not all of which I could attribute to the hangover. I fueled that anguish by surfing the web and reading the outcries on Facebook, stoking my fury and outrage until finally, a real desire to leave took over, to move out of the country and let the Trump supporters have it. I was done being involved, engaged, or caring at all.

Thoreau would have made his way to a peaceful spot in the woods and walked and contemplated what it all meant. Nature would help him find his answers. Hillary Clinton was found hiking in the woods very soon after the election, and President Obama said when trying to reassure his staff and the world on the morning after the election, "The sun will come up."

I was working on a documentary film at the time called *The End: Inside the Last Days of the Obama White House.* We were filming from election night through the transition, to see what it looked like inside the White House from the point of view of Obama's key staff, all of whom had been with him for eight years. When I initially looked at the footage of the President's calm admonishment that "The sun will come up," frankly, it irritated me. Why wasn't he angry? Or at least showing real disappointment, even horror, like the rest of us who oppose Trump and everything he stands for? I thought he should be telling us to fight.

But now, almost five months later, I understand what President Obama meant. And I think it's what Thoreau might have said, too. In "Civil Disobedience," he has a realization that *"if I put my head deliberately into the fire, there is no appeal to fire ... and I have only myself to blame"* and that we should resist, though we *"cannot expect, like Orpheus, to change the nature of the rocks and trees and beasts."*

Nature reminds us there are things we cannot change, and to rage against them is to struggle without reward. There is relief in understanding that we cannot change everything, and there is comfort in nature's cycles. With that relief comes clarity of focus. In my own walks/runs along the Hudson River in the woods near my home, and by pulling myself back from "the fire," I began to see what I could contribute, as a documentary filmmaker whose own family understands the terrible history of McCarthyism all too well.

As the name Roy Cohn began to resurface in the news, having been Trump's mentor and closest advisor and attorney for thirteen years, I saw a way that I could help reveal who Trump is: through a film that looked at Cohn and their friendship.

As my father said in my first film about my grandparents, Ethel and Julius Rosenberg, whom Cohn prosecuted in his first high-profile job as a young attorney, "I've always believed in exposure as a great kind of revenge."

My feeling now is that exposure can be a great weapon, and one that I'm uniquely equipped to employ. As Thoreau says, *"I can resist this to some effect."*

The sun came up on a new day when Trump became President. And it was still a beautiful, life-giving sun. This does not mean we do not resist; it means that we resist mindfully, we resist with focus, and we do not waste our strength resisting into the wind or against a rock or a tree that will not budge. Or as I did, into my pillow, my wine glass, and against a White House that stood solid and contained a person I could not remove, no matter how much I cried.

Photo credit: Adrianne Ryan

Holly Nadler has written for TV comedy shows, including Barney Miller *and* Laverne & Shirley. *She's had articles published in* Lear's *and* Cosmopolitan, *among other national magazines. Published books (Rowman & Littlefield) include* Haunted Island *and* Vineyard Confidential. *From her home on Martha's Vineyard, she's written thousands of stories for the* MV Times, *the* Vineyard Gazette, Cape Cod Magazine, *and the online newspaper* Martha's Vineyard Patch. *Her son, Charlie Nadler, is an aspiring screenwriter and standup comic living in New York. She currently lives with her second-born, a Boston Terrier named Huxley, in a deconsecrated library in Oak Bluffs.*

One of Several More Lives to Live

Holly Nadler

Let's say Henry David Thoreau was born on July 12, 1956. . . and he grew up in a tract development in southwestern Connecticut. When he learned, at his own precocious version of the age of five, that all the surrounding houses reiterated four identical designs, he collapsed on a mini-lawn, and bawled like a baby.

He made a deliberate plan to stay outside these pre-fab houses, even his own, and find solace in the meadows and woods beyond the subdivision — and thus began his love affair with nature.

In the third grade, he raised his hand when the teacher explained that President Lincoln had started the Civil War to free the slaves. Henry said in his piping eight-year-old voice, "But he didn't sign the Emancipation Proclamation until three years into the war. And that was because France and England refused to blockade Confederate ships unless he did."

The teacher, a prissy old broad, said, "Where did you get that information, Henry?"

That was easy: He'd been reading Will and Ariel Durant's history books from his dad's office, his dad being a history-professor-manqué turned lithium-battery manufacturer.

Young Henry was an active participant in the Civil Rights movement. In 1965, he tried to sign up for a bus headed for Selma, Alabama. The Presbyterian minister in charge of the trip said gently, "Henry, it's going to be too dangerous for a little kid." Dangerous? Well, that was a turn-off; he'd committed himself to non-violence when, in his kindergarten days, he read all he could about Mahatma Gandhi. So during the Selma operation, he stayed home and fasted, even going so far as to plunk his lunch money into panhandlers' cups on the walk home from school.

Starting in 1966, young Henry rode the train into Manhattan to take part in anti-Vietnam demonstrations. He met MLK and the preacher's good buddy, Thich Nhat Hahn, who was impressed with the eager 10-year-old, and persuaded him to meditate, which Henry did every day for the rest of his life.

And speaking of the rest of his life, he would have been spared, at the age of 44, the 19th-century death of tuberculosis. So let's say he lived at least all the way through the current political chaos. He'd written in the early 70s about his years in the woods of Chilmark on Martha's Vineyard, taking on a job as caretaker and resident hermit for a stockbroker who rarely visited. This time around, the two years, two months, and two days of the 19th century H.D. Thoreau morphed to 40 years and counting. He became agoraphobic, not about leaving his house, but departing the island. Every time he touched down in the real world, the sight of all the automobiles and factories, ugly signs, and ubiquitous McDonald's upset him mightily, and he found it easier to stay home.

Even from home, though, Henry found more publishing outlets than he would have in earlier times, especially online, for his splendid essays, so his fame equaled that of David Brooks, Michael Moore, and Robert Reich, the last of whom became a mentor of Henry's, launching him with his own podcast called, "First Take A Walk in the Woods!" He encouraged everyone to fight corporate America by giving up cars, shunning all but family-owned businesses, and cultivating vegetables, even in the tiny front yards of tract houses, something normally prohibited by the association's bylaws.

His chief mission was to encourage people to stop eating animals. He urged folks to stare into the eyes of any living creature to find a spark within each one, even brighter than the spark inside ourselves. (Once, Henry had shared a five-minute stare down into the gorgeous jade-green eyes of a preying mantis. The experience had left him in a state of grace for days). Henry said, "If you really pay attention, you'll feel how the absorption of animal flesh into your own flesh is gross and defiling."

Thoreau's 21st century contribution to mankind was to inspire people to stage their own nonviolent anarchy, even going so far as to cancel their electricity. "Don't wait for the United Nations and the Kyoto Treaty and your own government to solve climate change. Be the Spartacus or Joan of Arc of your own life by giving up cars, televisions, food sold in supermarkets. Finally, take up the mystic's path, pray without cease, and enter the eternal moment."

Now comes our current era with an orange ogre threatening to chomp democracy alive. Henry David Thoreau finds himself in a painful state. Henry's sensitivities are similar to those of canaries in the mine: he falls off his perch, dead (but revivable) and warns others of the toxic fumes. He marches, sends postcards by the hundreds, and leaves stunningly eloquent messages for senators, some of which make the front pages of major newspapers.

And then one day, during his millionth walk in the woods, and along Lucy Vincent Beach in Chilmark, he suddenly plops to the ground in the lotus position. It has occurred to him, in the parlance of a self-help book from the 1990s, that he's never really been that "INTO" this country.

It's not just the bad politics, the constant wars, and the recurrent and absurd hatred of immigrants as they become browner, but the sheer crappy aesthetics of the landscape and culture itself — the superhighways, the stinky, noisy traffic jams, the endless strip malls with identical franchises, and hundreds of square miles of suburbs — that impose a uniformity which sends Henry straight off his perch, dead. Again.

And now, at the age of 61, with decades of nonviolent resistance on his résumé and books and essays that have inspired

generations of "simplifiers," he wonders if he can fight any more.
There on the sands of Lucy Vincent — past the nudist part, so
he's re-donned his jeans and T-shirt — he recalls a fragment from
an old Bob Dylan song: "Honey, how come you don't move?"

But where would he go? He recalls how much he'd enjoyed
his junior year at the University of Edinburgh. Those cobbled
lanes. Ancient doorways and turrets and walkways above the
sea. He has some Scottish ancestry, and maybe his renown as an
American writer will enable him to get a long-term visa.

If he could make up his mind about his sexual orientation,
he might even marry a Scot of whatever gender, and stay
indefinitely. He ponders the grim weather. He's got a fierce case
of Seasonal Affective Disorder, but those long summer nights
when the city is limned with a starry white radiance …. ah!
Maybe Edinburgh can become his new Walden.

Yes, honey, time to move. Time to stop listening to the news that
always threatens to knock this canary to the littered floor of his
cage. He'll start fresh. Maybe even get off the Prozac.

"I left the woods for as good a reason as I went there. Perhaps it
seemed to me that I had several more lives to live, and could not
spare any more time for that one."

Photo credit: Pierre Chiha

John M. Nevison lives near Walden Pond. His most recent publication, "The Quiet Pattern of Walden Pond: Four models of the pond's water level," shows for the first time how the level of Walden varies through the seasons of the year, and is forthcoming in the Thoreau Society's "Concord Saunterer".

Avoiding Thoreau

John M. Nevison

It's been hard for me to avoid Henry David Thoreau, because for the past thirty-seven years my address has been 500 Thoreau Street, Concord, Massachusetts. From my front door to Thoreau's house site on Walden Pond is a fifteen-minute walk. And recently my doctor made me promise to take a thirty-minute walk each day.

Between my house and the pond is a steep rise known as Brister's Hill. In Thoreau's day, the base of Brister's Hill is where the farming fields ended and the sandy soil of the forest woodlots began. Emerson could see the beginning of the trees from his house in town. Today, the base of the hill is where Thoreau Street meets Walden Street at the entrance to the Concord-Carlisle Regional High School. Thoreau, the school teacher and naturalist, would be pleased to know that *Walden* is still taught in English classes, and be amazed at today's scientific understanding of our place in the cosmos.

I climb Brister's Hill on the woodland path beside Walden Street. Cars commuting to Boston speed up the hill beside me. Thoreau's reaction to today's automobile culture would be a big story.

At the top of the hill, I pause at the cellar hole where Brister Freeman's house once stood, and I envision the traces of his two stone fences extending fifty-seven yards to the east to meet at a point in the woods. Brister was a slave who grew up in Concord, fought in the Revolutionary War, won his freedom, and raised a family on this poor soil. Thoreau took time in *Walden* to notice several old apple trees that were all that remained of his farm.

I hear the roar of the four lanes of traffic ahead on Route 2. On the other side of the highway a sign says, "Walden Pond State Reservation." A smaller sign warns, "Not a public entrance," near the beginning of a woodland path that leads to the house site by the pond.

I decide not to take the path to Walden Pond. I bear east into the Hapgood Wright Town Forest, which contains Fairyland Pond. I follow a recently relabeled set of woodland trails that form a continuous path north from Thoreau's house site at Walden Pond to Emerson's house in the village. I wonder how Thoreau would react to seeing his name on an enamel disk on a tree that says, "Emerson-Thoreau Amble."

The Amble descends to Brister's Spring, which feeds Fairyland Pond. Thoreau knew the spring as a cool spot to have lunch on a hot summer's day. The water trickles out beneath the roots of a large oak and looks like an illustration from a child's fairy tale. Because I know that the spring's supply is an aquifer flowing north under the town dump and under Route 2, I hesitate to follow Thoreau's practice of dipping a cup of drinking water from the spring.

Beyond the spring, the trail runs level around a bend to Fairyland Pond itself. Thoreau would be surprised to see this "new" pond, which was constructed by his neighbors a few decades after his death. The fenced spillway in Fairyland's earthen dam is called a beaver deceiver and protects the drain from beavers' attempts to dam it up. Thoreau, who reported spotting a four-foot otter in these woods, would be glad to know that Concord wildlife persists and that his townsfolk are making an effort to coexist with it.

North of the pond, the trail forks at a wooden sign that says, "Amble." I leave the Amble to head west through a cathedral forest of white pines. The path emerges from the forest, crosses a level stretch of Walden Street, and heads into a large open meadow. This meadow protects an aquifer that forms part of the town's water supply. A red-tail hawk regularly surveys the field for mice. In October, when the meadow is full of milkweed and goldenrod, it hosts an annual butterfly census. Thoreau the surveyor would probably be pleased to see the multiple uses of precious town land he once measured.

Because it's getting dark, I survey the brush at the edge of the field for a patrolling coyote or a browsing deer. The meadow is quiet. The trail cuts diagonally across the field back towards my house on Concord's Thoreau Street. It is certainly difficult to avoid Thoreau in this part of the world. But maybe that's not such a bad thing.

Ashton Nichols is a regular contributor of nature essays to The Roost *blog at the Thoreau Farm and is the author of* Beyond Romantic Ecocriticism: Toward Urbanatural Roosting. *He is the Walter E. Beach '56 Distinguished Professor of Sustainability Studies and Professor of Language and Literature at Dickinson College. He spends his spare time in a stone cabin on the West Virginia-Virginia spine of the Blue Ridge, looking west.*

Henry David Builds His Hut

Ashton Nichols

I borrowed an axe to begin my hut.
It is always better to borrow than to buy,
For borrowing leaves only one axe
To be loaned, and after the loan, the return
Makes both borrower and lender feel good.
The lender feels good because he has loaned
His axe to a neighbor, and now that neighbor
Is a newfound friend. And the borrower feels good
Because he has gotten his house begun for free.

To buy an axe is to establish the need
For many more axes like the first one, since one
Buyer makes other people want to show off
The wealth and buy their own axe, too.
But then everyone buys an axe, and no one
Needs to borrow any more. Thus begins the
Path to no one ever needing to see his neighbor
At all, and thus is born the way for
Every soul to stay in his own house, with the
Window shutters closed up tight. A world full
Of borrowing is better than a world full of axes.

What else was I thinking about as I started
My hut? I thought a great deal about leaving home
To come away to these woods. There was mother
Back in Concord, just a mile and a half away.
I could walk home with ease. It would be easy to decide
To have dinner with her, or perhaps with
My best mentor and friend, Waldo Emerson. That

Is what I call him now. I have done so ever since
He said, "Henry David, from now on call me Waldo."

And I thought a lot about the town I left behind,
That Concord world of getting and spending,
As master Wordsworth says in one of his finest poems,
A world where men and women care more for money
Than for each other, a world where no one cares
As much for truth as for a life of things, or a life
Of his own loves. And those loves, even love for people,
But especially for things, are loves that do not matter.
Rather than love of money, or love of fame, or
Love of any man of woman, give me love of Truth.

So now it is time for me to get on with my hut,
For even though it is a warm summer day today,
The winter is cold, and winter will be coming on soon.

Barbara Olson is long-time fan of Henry and a senior docent at Thoreau Farm. She's a photographer and creator of a Walden Pond/Concord calendar. Now retired, Barbara loves having more time for swimming, hiking, and exploring new interests in nature.

What Would Henry Say?

Barbara Olson

If Henry came back for a day,
I think he'd have lots to say.
"Where is the loon,
Under the moon?
What happened, Walden, while I was away?"

He sat by the pond and pondered.
"Oh, no! Has this water been squandered?"
Now feeling some doubt.
"Is this really a drought?
Where is Goose Pond, where I wandered?"

He saunters for many a mile
To survey the woods for a while.
Ecstatic to see
So many more trees,
The offspring of "friends" bring a smile.

He crosses the road to view more.
"Wow! A glass house with many a door."
With awe on his face
He yells: "Finally a place!
A park in town with a bookstore."

Then seeing a lot full of cars
He feels like he's landed on Mars.
"Are these horses of tin?
And prisoners within?
I prefer to walk under the stars!"

Recall his past lectures in town?
Small crowds for the talk on John Brown.
Imagine his surprise,
With an audience size
That would now fill a ballpark in Beantown.

Henry spoke out long ago
That money was really a foe.
He was not delighted
With *Citizens United.*
People's justice hit a new low.

Remembering his past matriarch,
A family who carried a spark.
"They'd be proud to see
First Parish and me
Protesting a cause from the heart."

He loves the past from whence he came,
But now confused when called by name.
"If it's the future I see,
Who'd recognize me?
Oh, Lord, did my words bring me fame?"

Impressed that folks are truly unique.
"Go find what you intentionally seek.
There's plenty to write.
Take up your own fight.
Stop quoting me week after week!"

Sandra Harbert Petrulionis is Distinguished Professor of English and American Studies at Penn State University. She is the author of To Set This World Right: The Antislavery Movement in Thoreau's Concord, *the editor of* Thoreau In His Own Time, *and co-editor of other works on Thoreau and Transcendentalism. Although she read* Walden *in high school, no one introduced her to the militant Thoreau until graduate school, a deficiency she takes every opportunity to correct with her own students.*

Breaking the Law with Thoreau

Sandra Harbert Petrulionis

I'm going to adjust the verb tense. What *did* Henry Thoreau *do* as a political actor that still unsettles and emboldens us? In resisting the most urgent political crisis of his time — the enslavement of millions of fellow Americans — Thoreau broke the law, and he urges us to do the same.

Inspired by the activist example of his family and community, Thoreau shifted uneasily in deciding how best to oppose the travesty of slavery. When he stopped paying his poll tax to protest the Mexican War, which landed him in jail for a night, Thoreau's symbolic action was neither terribly original nor effective. His eloquent vindication of that action, however, laid down an ethic of individual "action from principle" that proved foundational for reformers long after his time. In "Resistance to Civil Government," Thoreau establishes that a tyranny of the majority kept the gears of the proslavery government "machine" well-oiled and running. But he opts out. "If the injustice . . . is of such a nature that it requires you to be the agent of injustice to another, then, I say, break the law. Let your life be a counter friction to stop the machine." It would be a hundred years before Americans fully seized the power of this defiant strategy, but Thoreau himself was just getting started.

Concord's proximity to the antislavery stronghold of Boston, in addition to the town's own radical contingent, made it a trusted stop on the Underground Railroad. Although few records document these encounters, we know that Thoreau flouted the federal Fugitive Slave Law by providing aid to at least three men and women who showed up at his family's door. Like all who defied this law, Thoreau risked up to six months in prison and $1,000 in fines (equivalent to roughly $30,000 in today's currency). His incendiary words matched his deeds when he took to the antislavery stage to speak on July 4, 1854, to explain that "our house was on fire." Castigating the spineless state and local authorities who had recently returned Virginian Anthony Burns to slavery, Thoreau exploded: "My thoughts are murder to the State, and involuntarily go plotting against her."

Five years later, Thoreau reached the pinnacle of his identity as a law-breaking opponent of the "machine." On December 3, 1859, the day after abolitionist zealot John Brown was hanged for attacking the federal arsenal at Harpers Ferry six weeks before, Thoreau relates in his Journal his morning's drive with a passenger he identified as "X." As Thoreau almost certainly knew, "X" (aka Francis Jackson Meriam) was one of the few of John Brown's men lucky enough to have made it out alive from the sensational scene at Harpers Ferry. On the day Thoreau took him safely from Concord to board a northbound train at the South Acton station, Meriam was still very much a wanted man, with a $500 reward on his head.

Let there be no doubt that Thoreau knew he was aiding and abetting a fugitive criminal. "When I hear of John Brown and his wife weeping at length, it is as if the rocks sweated," is his poetic ending to this day's Journal entry. After weeks of frenetic speaking in defense of Brown, Thoreau must have been thrilled to contribute to Brown's cause. He must also have suspected that if he had been caught helping Meriam escape, he would have been charged as an accessory after the fact to this notorious incident — in which case, it is not inconceivable that, like the six captured Harpers Ferry raiders, he would have been executed.

What did Thoreau do? When caught between the irreconcilable opposition of an individual's moral authority and the democratically supported law of the land, he repeatedly broke unjust laws. In so doing, he bequeathed to us an ethical compass by which we gain our bearings, one generation after another, and do the same.

John Pipkin grew up in Baltimore, Maryland and received his Ph.D. in English from Rice University. He currently lives in Austin, Texas, where he teaches creative writing and literature at Southwestern University and at the University of Texas. He also teaches in the Low-Residency MFA Program at Spalding University in Louisville, Kentucky. He is the recipient of fellowships from the Dobie Paisano Program, the Harry Ransom Center, the Mellon Foundation, and the MacDowell Colony. His first novel, Woodsburner, *which centered on a forest fire started by Henry David Thoreau in 1844, received widespread critical acclaim. His new novel,* The Blind Astronomer's Daughter, *is set in late-eighteenth-century Ireland, and was published by Bloomsbury in 2016.*

Henry David Thoreau and the "New Nationalism" of the Present Day

John Pipkin

Near the end of *Walden*, after many pages appreciative of the passing seasons and nature's magnificence — after all the wondrous minutiae that Thoreau carefully documents during his two years, two months, and two days at Walden Pond — he quotes the British poet William Habington and draws our attention to a wholly different landscape, the vast terrain hidden within us, a territory yet to be discovered and explored. Far from urging us to seek a hermit's refuge in the wilderness (as many misreadings of *Walden* would have us believe), the lingering message is that we should set out as pioneers in the exploration of ourselves.

> "Direct your eye right inward, and you'll find
> A thousand regions in your mind
> Yet undiscovered. Travel them, and be
> Expert in home-cosmography.

...Be rather the Mungo Park, the Lewis and Clark and Frobisher, of your own streams and oceans; explore your own higher latitudes... Nay, be a Columbus to whole new continents and worlds within you, opening new channels, not of trade, but of thought. Every man is the lord of a realm beside which the earthly empire of the Czar is but a petty state..."

And then, not unexpectedly, Thoreau turns to the political relationship that each of us — harboring worlds within ourselves — maintains with the state: "Yet some can be patriotic who have no self-respect, and sacrifice the greater to the less. They love the soil which makes their graves, but have no sympathy with the spirit which may still animate their clay. Patriotism is a maggot in their heads."

Patriotism is a slippery, prickly term, even in untroubled times (if there have ever been such), but seizing its meaning has never been more important than now, when the meaning of patriotism is too quickly conflated with the unyielding assumptions of nationalism and its obsession with myopic fantasies of former greatness. "Patriotism is a maggot in their heads." It is easy to take offense at what this statement seems to imply, and Thoreau excels at offending us when we would rather have truths served up simply, absolutely, unambiguously.

Patriotism troubles those who find themselves labeled unpatriotic. But patriotism is easily distinguished from nationalism. Nationalism is a rough-edged brick, better suited for throwing than for laying the foundations of improvement. Nationalism demands unbending loyalty, intolerance of any challenge to the state, a belief in some golden past when greater benefits were enjoyed by fewer participants in our democratic venture. Nationalism is marvelous fuel for pride, but it offers little food for progress.

Patriotism in Thoreau's formulation is demanding, strenuous, intellectual; it derives from a fundamental understanding of democracy's greatest asset: the individual.

In "Civil Disobedience," Thoreau tells us: "The progress from an absolute to a limited monarchy, from a limited monarchy to a democracy, is a progress toward a true respect for the individual." Ultimately, an enlightened democracy draws its power and authority from us. "There will never be a really free and enlightened State until the State comes to recognize the individual as a higher and independent power, from which all its own power and authority are derived, and treats him accordingly."

If the state is to be powerful, we must first discover our own power. If the state is to have authority, we must realize our authority as individual citizens. If the grand experiment in American democracy is to flourish, it must progress toward a true respect for the individual, and so as citizens we must insist that we are fully deserving of that respect. And how do we go about achieving this? Not just by exploring the shores of Walden Pond (though this may indeed offer a helpful prelude), but by exploring unfamiliar and uncomfortable regions of thought, by becoming experts in home-cosmography — mapping the vast, unknown universe within ourselves.

But if this is true patriotism — if this is the way of progress, of promoting a democracy respectful of and subservient to its citizens, then, oh, how arduous a task! How much simpler to do what we are told without question or reflection! How much easier to accept the state as superior to our unexplored selves and call this submission patriotic! But that is the patriotism Thoreau calls a "maggot in the head;" not content to feed upon the body, it feeds on living thoughts as well. It is not patriotic at all. Lack of self-knowledge — the absence of self-respect — makes us into weak citizens, engendering a weak state through easy indifference.

Thoreau would not at all be shocked to see the current conditions of our polarized politics. In "Civil Disobedience," he already suspected that "all voting is a sort of gaming," and for this reason, "a wise man will not leave the right to the mercy of chance." Patriotism requires more than voting, more than simply playing by the rules.

Thoreau didn't just foresee the possibility of our current crisis, he witnessed it in his own time. This is why he urges readers, then and now, to lay claim to patriotism before it can become a maggot in their heads, to make patriotism an active endeavor — not merely a label — a commitment to improving our democracy by challenging, questioning, and if necessary, resisting it, and this is only possible if we also strive to know and respect the best versions of ourselves.

Richard Primack, a professor at Boston University, investigates the effects of a warming climate on plants, birds, and insects using historical records, modern observations, and experiments. He is the author of Walden Warming: Climate Change Comes to Thoreau's Woods.

Is Climate Change Really Happening in Concord?

Richard B. Primack

In the 1850s, Henry David Thoreau observed the first flowers on Concord's wild blueberry shrubs in the middle of May. Now Concord residents see blueberry flowers in April, three to six weeks earlier than Thoreau.

Over the past fourteen years, my colleagues and I have repeated and built on the observations of Thoreau and other Concord naturalists. We have found that as global warming and urbanization raise temperatures in eastern Massachusetts, Walden Pond thaws earlier in late winter, trees leaf out and plants flower earlier in the spring, butterflies fly earlier, and many bird species arrive earlier along their spring migrations. We have also learned that our warming climate has contributed to the decline and disappearance of well-known wildflowers in Concord; roughly one-quarter of the plant species that Thoreau saw during his wanderings around Concord's woods and wetlands are no longer there. The changes we see in the climate and environment of Concord are a local version of the changes happening worldwide.

But some say, "So what? What is so wrong about a warming climate? In New England, earlier springs and warmer weather sound nice."

Warmer temperatures may be nice in many ways, but they bring problems, too. For example, many plants and animals in Concord are not suited to the new climate, and will decline and disappear. Rare and endangered species are particularly vulnerable as conditions change and as new species (including pests and diseases) arrive to take advantage of warmer temperatures. People are in danger, too. Rising sea levels, an indirect result of warming temperatures, will require tens or hundreds of billions of dollars to repair flood damage, to help people and businesses relocate, and to build new sea walls and dikes in areas where retreat is not feasible.

Away from New England, the problems of climate change will be even more severe. Huge areas of the United States, South Asia, Africa, and Southern Europe are already experiencing water shortages and droughts, leading to agricultural declines (collapse in some places) and water rationing for cities and industries. Further, heat waves caused by climate change increase the mortality rate of human populations, particularly for the people who are elderly, sick, or poor.

Earlier flowering and spring ice-out at Walden Pond are among the first warning signs of an impending global disaster.

Could Thoreau show us a better path?

Were Thoreau alive today, he would recognize climate change as one of the most pressing issues of our time. He would recognize the deep moral wrong of continuing climate-changing behaviors that harm people, plants, and animals. He would advise us to lead materially simple lives, take moral responsibility for our decisions and actions, and minimize our contributions to the fossil fuel emissions and rising levels of carbon dioxide that are largely responsible for climate change.

Thoreau would recognize the need for social and political action to address such a complex, far-reaching, and deep-seated problem as climate change. He would advocate for practical, immediate, and common sense approaches to reducing greenhouse gas emissions, rather than elaborate technological fixes for the distant future. For example, Thoreau would favor infrastructure, policies, and cultural norms that encourage the use of small, fuel-efficient cars, public transportation, and bicycles. He would encourage people to use less energy in their homes and businesses and would advocate for government programs that do the same.

In addition, Thoreau would encourage us to walk in natural places and observe what is there; we should learn the names and characteristics of the birds, mammals, plants, and other species. As we do, we will understand nature better, and be better advocates for its protection. We will "see" climate change and its impacts. We, like Thoreau, should be citizen scientists; we should gain and share insights from the natural world and become more effective thinkers and communicators.

From walking on the shores of Walden Pond and recording the flowering of blueberry bushes in early April, a month earlier than Thoreau had seen them a century and a half ago, climate change became real for me in a way that it wasn't before. I saw climate change. Thoreau would encourage us all to do the same. He would encourage us to take action. Now.

Robert D. Richardson is an American historian and biographer. He is the author of Henry David Thoreau: A Life of the Mind, *as well as* William James: In the Maelstrom of American Modernism; *and* Emerson: The Mind on Fire. *He is married to author Annie Dillard.*

What Would Henry Do in 2017?

Robert D. Richardson

We don't need to ask what Henry would do in 2017. We know what he did when he faced government actions he thought so wrong that they were potentially capable of destroying the country.

"It is not desirable," said he, "to cultivate a respect for the law, so much as for the right."

And he also said: "This people must cease to hold slaves, and to make war on Mexico, though it cost them their existence as a people."

He refused to pay his poll tax, he went (briefly) to jail, and above all *he spoke up*, writing at length and often against slavery, against the Mexican War, and in favor of old John Brown.

No, the question in 2017 is not what would Henry do; that's settled. The question is what will I do? What will you do?

Tammy Rose is a Waltham-born, Brooklyn-based playwright and artist. Her Concord series of plays include Sense, Thoreau v. Shultz, *and* Transcendental Ghosts of Fairyland Pond. *She also has an MBA and an MS in Human Factors in Information Design, and, usually, a day job.*

"Lemme Tell You What I Would Do..." A Henry Monologue

Tammy Rose

A single stool stands center stage, next to a microphone, both lit by a spotlight. We are in a giant theater. There are no other signs of life, either backstage or even in the audience, other than Henry, a lone figure, pacing in the wings like a tiger. He has a grizzled beard and a slightly unkempt look, which may be insanity, genius, or George Carlin. He enters from stage right.

Henry:

Alright, you are gonna come across a lot of great ideas in these pages of what Henry would do. The "great and holy" Henry David Thoreau. Harrumph!! None of those are me. All of us are just figments in the minds of others — I'm just one figment of many. A fellow ain't got a soul of his own, just a little piece of a big soul, the one big soul that belongs to everybody,

So lemme tell you what I would do.

Now, I'm just a guy. A writer. A FAILED writer. A failed teacher. Based on what I see of your society, I think there are PLENTY of people like me who go out to find their own Walden cabin in the woods, and discover that it is nothing more than a cardboard box sitting on a heat vent in the city.

That's probably where I'd be in this society, a gentleman of a certain age. Probably forcibly retired. No savings or family to fall back on. My so-called genius never appreciated in my lifetime. Which I expect is true for a lot of you out there.

Honestly? I'd do what I always did. I'd saunter, like before, four hours or more. Then I'd come home and write, then I'd publish, and then I'd get mad as hell and refuse to take it any more. Lather, rinse, and repeat.

I'd saunter, hell, I would MARCH. I'd march for Women's Rights, I'd march in Selma, I'd go on the Salt March in India. I'd sit at whatever lunch counter I needed to, I'd party all night in a dance club in Orlando and fight for everyone to use any bathroom they choose and marry whomever they choose. I'd fight for the right for people to live their own lives the way they choose. It's never too late to show up.

I'll be all around in the dark – I'll be everywhere. Wherever you can look – wherever there's a fight, so hungry people can eat, I'll be there. Wherever there's a cop beatin' up a guy, I'll be there. I'll be in the way guys yell when they're mad. I'll be in the way kids laugh when they're hungry and they know supper's ready, and when the people are eatin' the stuff they raise and livin' in the houses they build – I'll be there, too.

I'd call bullshit every time I hear anyone use a bullshit slogan. It can't happen here! War is peace. Freedom is slavery. Ignorance is strength. Alternative facts. I wouldn't be shy. I'd talk to Gandhi and Martin Luther King, Jr. and Trayvon Martin. And I would hope to God I'd have the courage to get in the way of the bullets.

I'd pitch my camp, my cardboard box, or my teepee out in front of the biggest institution I could find. Instead of living in the woods, observing nature and all its beauties, I would go out into the world and observe humans in all their evils. I would keep a diary, a journal, and several social media accounts. I would teach history, every way that history repeats and how it rhymes. And every time people stopped listening, I would ring the bells of every cathedral I could find.

And I would hope that all of you would fight for truth, justice and . . . I'd like to include "the American way," but I don't know what that is anymore. You don't need me, you don't need Superman. Be your own friggin' hero.

Henry drops the mic.

Henry references the following works:

Lewis, Sinclair. *It Can't Happen Here.* UK: Penguin, Penguin Random House, 2017 (1935).

Network. Film. Dir. Sidney Lumet. United Artists, 1976.

Orwell, George. *1984.* New York: Penguin, 1992 (1949).

Steinbeck, John. *The Grapes of Wrath.* New York: Penguin Classics, 1992 (1939).

And Superman.

Photo credit: Frank Serpico

Frank Serpico is a retired New York City police detective who in the 1970s exposed widespread corruption in the New York City Police Department. A best-selling book by Peter Maas entitled Serpico *chronicled his police exploits, resulting in a movie by the same name starring Al Pacino. Frank is now an animal and civil rights activist and recipient of the 2001 Jolene Marion Memorial Award for the Advancement of Animal Law, and the New York Police Department's Medal of Honor.*

My Walden

Frank Serpico

How many times have you led me into the wood?
And I attended as best I could.

Oh Henry, since you left, there are no "new lands to find,"
just those you left behind, preserved and respected.
No new creatures to be found; only those that remain protected.
The fair landscapes you have seen may never be seen again
and "… the only permanent shore" may soon be seen no more.

Oh Henry David, where are the cliff swallows that once flew
an aerial ballet, for young and old to view?
They no longer return to the cliff by the river.
Their nesting place pillaged.
On my little piece of wetland marked by a surveyor's pin
bulldozed by builders: "The result will be that he will perchance
get a little more money to hoard."
Where is that gnarly old mulberry tree, laden with berries
to feed our feathered family?

Victims of the builder's saw, an old cottonwood, a wild cherry
in its infancy, and a dozen more by the stream where the
heron fed.
The muskrat and the beaver have fled.

The builder wanted a better view of the river.
Too much in haste to waste a walk across the road to have a
closer view?
On my deeded land that I had planned to be forever wild.
A globally rare habitat sprinkled still with arrowheads.

Meanwhile, the builder loudly brags about
how his only son was an Eagle Scout.

Oh Henry, who is there to keep the destruction at bay,
While DEC and local government look the other way?
Environmental Neanderthals, I say!

The only green they understand is what can be folded and
slipped in their extended hand.
Never has justice been in greater need.
They have desecrated my Walden with their greed.

Oh Henry, life without principle is not worth living.
Yet, somehow the race survives.
But what will remain for the young?
What is there left for those that follow?

First the cliff and then the swallow.

I live in a cabin in the wood
In the bucolic little hamlet of Stuyvesant on the Hudson.

Bald eagles soar overhead.
Ruby throated humming birds sip nectar in my garden.

The town was named after Peter Stuyvesant, the last Dutch
Governor of New York who said at the time,
"The people are growing strange in their ways and loose in
their morals."
But that was over 400 years ago!

Today little has changed as you drive along pastured
farmlands; bike through fields of towering corn.
The air is sweet with the scent of wildflowers and fresh cut hay.
Yet, something somewhere emits a stench, a foul odor of decay,
pervasive yet elusive, no doubt emitting from a rotting
carcass, a dead skunk or an open door at the village town hall.

Oh Henry, the state you imagined does not yet exist "… to be just
to all men and to treat the individual with respect as a neighbor."

Photo credit: Corrine H. Smith

Corinne H. Smith is a writer, poet, and outdoor educator. She is the author of Westward I Go Free: Tracing Thoreau's Last Journey, *the first book to follow his 1861 trip from Massachusetts to Minnesota, as well as a biography for middle schoolers,* Henry David Thoreau for Kids: His Life and Ideas, with 21 Activities. *She currently divides her time between Pennsylvania and Massachusetts where she serves as an interpreter and blog writer for Thoreau Farm.*

Dancing on the Eights

Corinne H. Smith

A series of unusual circumstances once turned one of my personal heroes into a temporary time traveler. I ended up sequestering Henry David Thoreau at my lakeside home for six weeks. It was an eye-opening experience for both of us.

Henry embraced some parts of my lifestyle and disdained others. When it came to watching and accepting television, though, I wasn't sure which way he would go. I explained the technology to him as best as I could. And to be polite, I cut down on my viewing hour, except for my football-watching binges on Sundays, of course. Henry soon learned not to jump in alarm each time I yelled at the little men in the glowing box.

One day I was scheduled to run an outdoor program at our nature center in the afternoon, and I needed to know when the rain was expected to arrive. I turned on the TV to The Weather Channel. Immediately the room filled with urgent voices. The forecasters warned that lines of tornadoes would pass through Arkansas today.

I tapped down the sound and described the situation to Henry. He stared at the screen in fascination, grasping the concept of satellite-based weather tracking. When "Local on the 8s" appeared, we watched as more benign green blotches headed toward our own county on the screen. A light piano melody played in the background. "You have much music in this world of yours," Henry said. "And the rain seems to march in time with it." He was right. I'd never noticed this before.

I made a move to turn off the set, but Henry reached out to stay my hand. His eyes never left the screen. "This interests me. I should study it more."

"Okay with me," I said. I laid the remote on the coffee table. "The red button turns it off." He nodded, without turning. I picked up my bag and left for the day.

When I returned much later, I was stunned to see that Henry was still sitting on the couch, staring at the screen. "Did you stay in here all day?" I asked. I already saw the answer, over in the kitchen. The cider jug was almost empty. The loaf of bread and the jars of peanut butter and jelly had been seriously invaded, too. At least he remembered to eat.

Henry focused on me, then looked around. "I suppose so. But see what the tornadoes did!" He pointed. The footage was tragic. Buildings were crushed. Cars were piled in impossible places. It was hard to watch, yet even harder to look away. "Can you believe that no one was killed?" he asked. "This is fabulous to me."

I knew he was using the older definition of the word, to mean something incredible or astounding. "Wow. Yes, it's terrible," I said. "You've never seen this kind of storm damage yourself?"

He shook his head. "Not in Massachusetts, no. But it would indeed make a remarkable study: to determine wind direction and velocity and the path of the storm, as these people and pictures have shown." His face was serious enough, but his eyes shone at the scientific prospects. If he had the means, I thought, he'd be headed to Arkansas himself to do some exploring and thinking on his own.

When the commercials came on, he muted them with a practiced hand, mimicking my own example. But as soon as "Local on the 8s" appeared, he pushed the button again. "The best part of all!" he cried. This time a jazzy tune filled the air. Henry was suddenly on his feet, dancing a freeform jig. As the weather map gave way to the three-day forecast, Henry was spinning across the room, with arms and legs flailing. Before I knew it, he grabbed my hand and twirled me around. I laughed, trying to match his style. Our merriment lasted only a minute. Then we were abruptly whisked back to the reality of the power of Nature.

For the rest of the afternoon and into the evening, we seesawed between tragedy and gaiety, the storms and the music. I finally put an end to it when I was too tired to move. But this day marked the beginning of what would become a semi-regular routine for us. Who knew that he was such a good dancer?

I learned a lot while Henry Thoreau was here. I cherish the memories of our walks and our talks and being able to hear his ideas in his own voice. I respect him even more than I ever did before. But now that he's gone? It's the weather dancing that I miss the most.

*Richard Smith is an independent scholar and historian. Since
1999, he has written and lectured on Thoreau's life and times.
Through his work as a living history interpreter, Richard can often
be seen portraying Thoreau in Concord and around the country
at schools, churches, libraries, and universities.*

The Politics of Action

Richard Smith

Henry Thoreau had a very dim view of politicians. While it is true that much of society came under Thoreau's scrutiny — reformers, philosophers, poets, and the "mass of men" in general — he often described politics and politicians in the harshest of terms.

"The majority of the men of the North, and of the South and East and West are not men of principle," he wrote in 1854.

Thoreau never belonged to any political party. He was neither Democrat nor Whig. In fact, there is no record of Thoreau ever voting. He viewed politics as "superficial and inhuman" and even wrote that anything having to do with politics never "concerned me at all." Transcendentalist that he was, Thoreau believed in the power of the individual to change society, not organizations, and certainly not politicians or political parties.

Still, this non-involvement in political affairs didn't stop Thoreau from commenting on the politics of the day, and ante-bellum America was full of issues that affected — and threatened — the very existence of the United States.

The major issue in Thoreau's day was, of course, slavery. In his 44 years, he saw the "peculiar institution" expand and become the number one factor in the United States' economic growth. While many Northerners (perhaps naively) viewed slavery as a Southern issue, Thoreau and other Abolitionists were well aware that the Northern economy, in particular the textile mills of New England, were thriving because of the cotton that was produced with slave labor.

While Thoreau stayed away from politics, that did not stop him from being an involved citizen.

"The fate of the country does not depend on how you vote at the polls ... but on what kind of man you drop from your chamber into the street every morning," he wrote.

It is a popular misconception today that Thoreau spent most of his time being a hermit at Walden Pond, but this could not be farther from the truth. He was very much involved in national affairs, especially as an anti-slavery advocate.

Thoreau famously went to jail in 1846 for not paying his poll tax because he did not want his money supporting a government that supported slavery, and he explained this position in "The Relation of the Individual to the State," a lecture which later became "Civil Disobedience." He publicly spoke out several times against slavery, notably in his lecture "Slavery in Massachusetts," delivered in 1854, and in his "Plea for Captain John Brown," in 1859.

And Thoreau was a well-known conductor on the Underground Railroad. While he disparaged politics and politicians, he took an active role in standing up against what he viewed as the country's wrongs.

This is the Henry Thoreau we can learn from today. At a time when our nation seems to be again divided, perhaps we need to take a closer look at Thoreau's activism. He knew that in a democracy it was the will of the people that ruled, and that politicians work for us.

What would Thoreau do today with the current climate of divisive politics and rampant human rights violations?

I believe that he would take an active part in trying to make the government understand that he was unhappy with the way things were being run. Yes, he signed petitions in his day. Perhaps he would do so today. He would maybe even be active on social media in order to get his point across.

As the 1850s wore on, and the expansion of slavery became an even more urgent matter for abolitionists, some believed that more drastic measures were needed to fight slavery. "Breaking unjust laws" became the norm: hiding runaway slaves, openly engaging slave catchers, boycotting Southern goods. All were used as weapons against a government he viewed as immoral. Perhaps that is what Thoreau would do today. He believed that it is our duty as citizens to let the government know that it is doing things we disagree with — and if such a government failed to listen to words, then direct action might be required to get its attention. He stood up to a racist government by breaking the law. Perhaps he would view today's administration's "Muslim bans" as also being racist. He saw a government enact policies that squelched human rights. Perhaps he would see the same sort of human rights violations going on today. Would he speak out? Would he break immoral laws? I believe that he would.

One hundred and fifty years later, we can learn a lot from Thoreau. Speak out against the government. Stand up to policies that you don't like. Petition, march, contact your representatives. Thoreau knew that an individual can force change. It is our government, and it is up to us to affect the change we want.

In his essay "Slavery in Massachusetts," he wrote: "The law will never make men free; it is men who must make the law free."

A longtime teacher at Concord Academy (now retired), Sandy Stott wrote for and edited Thoreau Farm's blog, The Roost, *for over four years, during which he found the truth of his short essay presented here reinforced over and over. During the 90s, he edited the journal* Appalachia, *and he continues to write for the journal as an essayist and its Accidents Editor. His book on search and rescue in the White Mountains will be published by University Press in New England in 2018.*

What Henry Did

Sandy Stott

It is near the Ides of October, and here in the northeast, our annual descent steepens; many of us now rise in darkness and head home in twilight. Even as the trees pulse scarlet and yellow, even as the sky is often achingly blue, we feel an inward turn; we tend toward hunker.

All of this is seasonal backdrop for a fractious, troubled world — our politics are those of clamor and calamity, we arm against ourselves, we seem to outnumber the very earth. In such a season, at such a time, many of us search for hope, for a voice that both admits and admires complexity and sees still through the turmoil to the delight of life, to a daily goodness and purpose.

For me and for many, such a voice carries over the years from Henry David Thoreau, whose 200th birthday on July 12, 2017, nears. How is it that a man dubbed by many as misanthropic and hypocritical, a man often perceived to be a hermit, a man who never "made it" in his era and died young, offers such a lasting uplift for those of us who read him, and then often follow him out the door?

Perhaps there is a simple answer... with a complex explanation: in his mid-20s, as Henry Thoreau sought purpose and traction in his hoped-for life as a writer, he took on an assignment for the short-lived Transcendental journal, *The Dial*. In the resulting essay, "The Natural History of Massachusetts," Thoreau's early foray into the style and content that would form his life's work, he wrote the following passage:

"Surely joy is the condition of life. Think of the young fry that leap in the ponds, the myriads of insects ushered into being on a summer evening, the incessant note of the hyla with which the woods ring in the spring, the nonchalance of the butterfly carrying accident and change painted in a thousand hues upon its wings, or the brook minnow stoutly stemming the current, the luster of whose scales worn bright by attrition is reflected upon the bank."

Almost twenty years later, as he lay dying at age 44, Thoreau worked on his final essay, "Autumnal Tints", a look at the leaves and the flaring season that ushers in the annual deaths of the world. A reader might expect dark tints, a gathering gloom; instead, affirmation rises the way light rises, sometimes unexpectedly, from the leaves lying on the dark forest floor. Sometimes in fall, your way is limned by these footlight leaves; light both falls from the sky and rises from the ground; the day is suffused with it. In "Autumnal Tints", we find that joy is still the condition of life... and even death.

That, I think, is Henry Thoreau's sustaining, daily vision, a vision he kept choosing, even in the face of wasting disease. It survived a world as fractured as ours; it survived also Thoreau's own ferocious intelligence, capable of such piercing social criticism that it reads as fresh today; it survived every descent, even his own. For all of us "carrying accident and change painted in a thousand hues upon [our] wings," such a vision can hold daily darkness at bay; we can work forward in its spirit and find the abiding beauty and joy of this world.

That's what Henry Thoreau did.

Libby Wagner is a poet, author, and speaker. She is the author of The Influencing Option: The Art of Building a Profit Culture in Business *(2010),* What Will You Do With Your 90,000 Hours? The Boardroom Poet's Thoughts on Work *(2016), and three collections of poems, including* Like This, Like That *(2002),* Somehow *(2012), and the forthcoming* Dancing on the Summer Lawn. *Collaborating with Irish musician and composer Owen Ó Súilleabháin, they've created* Harvest *(2015), an audio collection of poems and original music, and the genre-breaking* Now Just This *(2017), an embodied experience of spoken word poetry.*

Now This: A Thoreau Reflection

Libby Wagner

My first real memory of Thoreau was in a college class called "American Life Through Thought". It was a special honors class taught by the program director and my favorite teacher, John Kleber. Morehead, Kentucky, with its rolling hills and brilliant deciduous autumns, is nestled in the foothills of the Appalachian Mountains. I became enamored with the unique Scots-Irish culture, the hammered dulcimer music, traditional story-telling, and homespun crafts of nearby Berea College. We read the American Transcendentalists Emerson and Thoreau, and I remember Kleber's admiration for these writers, who were not only reflecting on their times but also blazing a path for modern American literature. In *Walden*, my favorite chapter was "Where I Lived and What I Lived For."

> *"I went to the woods because I wished to live deliberately, to front only the essential facts of life and see if I could not learn what it had to teach, and not, when it came to die, discover that I had not lived . . . . I wanted to live deep and suck the marrow of life . . ."* — *Walden*

One day in particular set me on my path, personally and professionally. We left campus and piled into a bunch of cars heading east near Cave Run Lake. I sat in the back seat, unbuckled and swaying left and right in a boat of a late 70s Impala. Pink Floyd played on a cassette tape, the sun moved in and out of high cumulus clouds. I remember thinking my teacher was cool, and weird, and maybe not so old as I'd imagined from my twenty-year-old vantage-point.

We walked through the woods together, a small group of twelve, mostly non-hikers. Two classmates were "the Boy Scouts," who swaggered with what seemed like excessive gear to me: machetes, bulky coiled ropes over their shoulders, and canteens bumping against their hips. The walk was long, without a path. We were invited not to talk, until scaling a hillside provided a good reason for those ropes and the Boy Scouts' wilderness skills, and we needed more than hand signals.

Prior to that walk, I do not remember a time when I had been encouraged to walk silently anywhere. Here in the woods, I began to notice the natural world in an entirely different and reverent way.

It was dark when we returned, scraped and scratched. No Pink Floyd on the way back, just the deepening skies and the fireflies racing past the windows.

Only recently have I understood the golden thread stitching so many elements of my life to that Thoreau walk. After graduation, I moved to South Florida, where I taught English in a suburb of Ft. Lauderdale. Since American Literature was the approved curriculum for Junior English, I taught *To Kill a Mockingbird, Catcher in the Rye*, and parts of *Walden.* I dragged my students out in the mid-day heat with their journals to sit in the dirt, write, and reflect. Years later, I taught a one-credit hiking class on the Olympic Peninsula in Washington State. On the weekends, we drove winding roads to hike along river valleys, wild beaches, and rainforest paths. Back in the English classroom again, we read "Where I Lived" and David James Duncan's *The River Why.*

"Thoreau is not fast food literature," I'd say. "You have to read it slowly and savor it."

Over and over, I would go to the woods. I would meet my future husband on a back-country planting crew. I would spend five or ten days in the wilderness and watch the Rolodex of my life fall away. I would get down on my knees to replant sedges, leutkea, and lupines. I'd drink cowboy coffee from an aluminum cup and watch the night sky, the northern lights and the sandstone cliffs turn pink at dawn. I could place my boots on a worn path and trust the strength of my legs. I could feel my heart beat with each step. I was awake and alive in my meandering. I know if I don't go to the woods regularly, some essential and divine part of me begins to wither. My ritual, whether alone, with friends, or with students, is to drive in silence to our wilderness destination. Once, outside Leavenworth and the North Cascades, I invited a group of colleagues to stop talking as we drove the last hour to Icicle Creek.

"This is my church," I said to my colleagues, perhaps an odd request from their point of view but, though it was the first time I'd said it aloud, I had suddenly realized it was true.

Before I turned fifty, many friends and family offered their advice about how to mark such an occasion with a party or celebration or holiday. But nothing sounded right. About a month before, I drove to meet some friends near Paradise on Mt. Rainier, a few hours south of Seattle. When I got to Ashford just outside the park and saw the evergreens rise tall and dark, mysterious as a cathedral, I knew where I wanted to be on my birthday: in the woods. When I learned my sister's cancer was back and she was indeed dying, I went to the woods. When my heart was broken beyond repair, I needed to feel my body on the earth and the sunlight sifting through tree branches.

A few years ago, I found myself outside of Concord, Massachusetts. My schedule as a speaker and consultant has me in planes and hotels, and at times, I feel as if I am "living meanly like ants." So there I was, deep into my schedule, when I was struck: *Walden.* There was no way to come this far from my Seattle home and not go to Thoreau's place.

It was late in the afternoon, an uncharacteristically warm February day. The parking lot across from the pond was mostly empty. I had no proper hiking shoes or clothes, and took only my notebook and camera. Quietly, I walked along the path and around the small pond. I smelled the wet earth. I wondered at its

potential for lushness in the summer. The winter branches were
bare and the sun hung low in the sky. It was almost dark and the
park closed when I returned to my car.

It's hard to imagine when I'm walking along East 81st Street in
Manhattan or riding the water taxi toward the Seattle skyline on
a misty morning what Thoreau would've made of this complex
and "advanced" modern world. I suspect he seemed odd and a
little weird in his own time, and that perhaps his questions and
answers would still be found back in the woods.

In my own work, which typically takes the form of poem, I'm
forever writing my Thoreau poem. I wrestle with the juxtaposition
of the life of the spirit and the life of the body. I question what
it means to "live deliberately." I'm forever finding my connection
to and observation of the natural world as solace and answer, as
philosophy and religion: the seasonality is all.

The only answer worth knowing is that things change. And the
human stretch between birth, delight, heartbreak, and death
washes over us again and again. Sometimes the woods are my
back garden above the Puget Sound, or a walk around nearby
Green Lake. Sometimes it's the magic of the Grove of Patriarchs'
massive old growth cedars at the base of Mt. Rainier. The woods
have been the answer and the call and the question. It's the only
truth I know, my salvation.

*Laura Dassow Walls is the William P. and Hazel B. White
Professor of English at the University of Notre Dame, where
she teaches courses in American literature, American
Transcendentalism, and environmental humanities. She has
published widely on Thoreau, Emerson, and Alexander von
Humboldt, among others; she hopes her most recent book,* Henry
David Thoreau: A Life *(University of Chicago Press, 2017)
will help inspire others to take a fresh look at America's iconic
environmental writer and philosopher.*

"What Would Thoreau Do?"

Laura Dassow Walls

The first thing Thoreau would do is put down the newspaper, turn off his computer, put away his cell phone, and step out for a long walk. He'd take along his notepad, or, depending on the season, his flute. He might bring along a friend, perhaps a child — though he'd instruct her to look, not talk, along the way. But heading home, he'd likely stop to chat— with a farmer in his field, a boy fishing in the river, a friend on the street — to share some marvel he'd found: an arrowhead, a seed pod, a flower just coming into bloom. He'd ask how their crops were doing, what they'd caught lately, how deep the snow was out their way. They might even argue politics. And once home, he'd write up his notes, describing with care the flavor of his life on that particular day, seen, heard, felt, scented, tasted, the season's inner and outer weather, turning an eye to the deeper patterns, the higher questions, gleaming through the most common moments.

There'd be chores to do and he'd do them, the dinner table to grace with conversation, and if, that evening, he heard someone playing the piano in the parlor, he'd come downstairs from his study to join in a song, perhaps even dance. Or there might be a lecture that evening; he'd go with family and friends to listen to what the speaker had to say. Whatever the topic — geography, chemistry, natural history or the history of religion; women's rights, abolitionism, civil resistance — they'd ask questions and argue it over afterwards, too, back in the parlor. Or perhaps he'd be the one giving the lecture that night, advancing his thoughts in conversation with his neighbors, or traveling to a nearby village lyceum. He'd ask them to think about life's essentials: wild apples or autumn leaves, the ethics of hunting, how to walk into the wind, what it would profit them to gain the world and lose their own soul. For he knew that every town and village is a university where we learn from and teach each other under the skies of our common home.

At times, Thoreau would brace himself to face his nation's latest moral earthquake: in his day, it was the invasion of Mexico, the rendition of a fugitive slave, the popular condemnation of John Brown. Each time he would force himself to a moral reckoning so severe it might cast in doubt his very right to walk into nature at all. This reckoning would begin with the soul-searching he demanded in "Civil Disobedience": Have I, in my actions, lent myself to this injustice? If so, I must change my life — for words are barren unless joined with deeds.

Next he would ask: Have I anything to say that others should hear? There were times when he judged himself unready to speak out. But when he believed others spoke wrongly and his own thoughts must be heard, he would write furiously through the day, and at night keep pencil and paper under his pillow. Once his deliberations were complete, he would step fearlessly before the public, trusting his own moral courage to defend what he believed to be true, and trusting his listeners to hear him out with respect, talk it through afterward, and act on what they decide is right. For they would be, all of them, engaged in composing a good common world together, and that's what it takes. Then he would push to publish his words to the world, so the widest possible audience could weigh them. Only in this way would the ethics of the wider community be challenged, tested, and affirmed in the cause of social justice.

And then he would put down the newspaper, put away his computer, turn off his cell phone, and step out for another long walk, notepad in hand; for in the beauty of nature, even the broken nature that was Concord in his day, he found the hope that sustained him against despair. And if anyone were to stop him along the way to ask, "But Henry, what should I do?," he'd fix them with his terrible searching eyes, and reply, "I can't tell you. What do you think you should do?"

Photo credit: Jim Coutre

Leslie Perrin Wilson is Curator of the William Munroe Special Collections at the Concord Free Public Library and a writer on local historical and literary topics. She has curated the CFPL's Thoreau bicentennial exhibition, "Concord, which is my Rome": Henry Thoreau and His Home Town, *on view in the library's gallery July-October 2017. She is also the author of* Picturing Emerson: An Iconography — *a collaboration with Joel Myerson.*

Would Thoreau Love Concord Now?

Leslie Perrin Wilson

If Henry Thoreau were to materialize in Concord today, he would likely recognize the contours of the town where he spent his life. While much has changed since he perambulated, observed, and wrote here, multiple threads connect the physical and social landscapes of Concord past and present.

Since Thoreau's death, many buildings have been demolished and replaced. Nevertheless, despite significant development, a sufficient number of antique buildings remain in Concord Center and more remote areas to preserve some appearance of the place in earlier times. Thoreau would probably censure the size and lavishness of recently-built houses and applaud the impulse to preserve durable, still-useful historic structures.

In the mid-nineteenth century, the landscape of Concord was more open than it is today — the result of sustained and intensive wood-cutting. Thoreau would notice an increase in vegetation overall, but would also observe and mourn the loss of native species. The local impact of climate change would underscore for him the danger of blindness to the complex relationship between man and nature. But the amount of open space preserved here would encourage his optimism in human ability to alter destructive behavior and allow him to pursue his essential daily walks.

Thoreau would also find aspects of the social landscape of Concord today familiar. In his time, the town had its share of affluent residents, as now, although the current concentration of wealth among ever-fewer people would probably trouble him. Thoreau's Concord boasted a relatively literate, well-educated population, as it still does. And, setting a precedent that has influenced the town to the present day, nineteenth-century Concord enfolded an unusually large number of intellectuals and writers, among whom were close friends of Thoreau.

But Thoreau valued humbler company, too. He would be disturbed by the decline of farmers and other hands-on workers, and by the prevalence of jobs that keep people indoors. Also, he might frown upon Concord's primary status as residential town rather than provider of concrete goods and essential services.

Concord's renown as a tourist site would probably also go against Thoreau's grain. Finding everything he needed here to fuel his own intellectual and spiritual explorations, he urged, "Take the shortest way round and stay at home." He disdained the notion of visitors making pilgrimages to places no better than their home turf for fueling higher pursuits, and promoted intense engagement with one's own corner of the world rather than looking elsewhere for inspiration and answers.

Thoreau might or might not have admired the commitment to community that so many Concordians practice nowadays. His love of place was intense but, in some ways, impersonal — at least as much philosophical as emotional — and he was never a ready joiner in common endeavors. As a political animal, he resisted overt activism unless extreme injustice — notably slavery — demanded it.

Would Thoreau weigh in on artificial turf on Concord's playing fields, single-serving plastic water bottles, or access to the Estabrook Woods? Would he display a Black Lives Matter sign on his front lawn? Although there is a local tradition of invoking his name in local debates, such questions can't be answered. Yes, much about Concord present is rooted in Concord past. Yes, we know how Thoreau reacted to concerns of his era. But the world beyond and including Concord has changed. Thoreau expressed himself at a particular moment in time, without foreknowledge of how the circumstances and contexts of future debate would evolve.

However a transported Thoreau might feel about Concord controversies right now, he would embrace the place in a clear-eyed fashion, just as it is. He criticized the town, but it was always central to his process of observation and discovery, the place where he could best expand his consciousness. To do so required deep, nuanced local knowledge and an ability to accept good and bad alike. He wrote, *"Here* . . . is all that you love, all that you expect, all that you are . . . Here is all the best and all the worst you can imagine. What more do you want?" (Journal, November 1, 1858). This approach transcends any specific issue at any particular time.

Anna West Winter is the executive director of the Concord-based non-profit organization Save Our Heritage. She serves on various boards including: The Walden Woods Project, Concord Museum, Louisa May Alcott's Orchard House, Emerson Hospital, Trustees of Reservations, and PBS Nova. She and her husband Neil live in Concord, where they raised their two children.

Soliciting a Saunter

Anna West Winter

It was a night like many others since November 8, 2016. Unrelenting daylight hours of haunting disbelief transitioned into bleak evening ritual: crying foul at cable news pundits while scrolling my iPhone for the latest Change.org petition to peruse. Steeling myself for yet another anxious sleep, my subconscious strained to travel to palliative surroundings. Mission not quite accomplished, I landed at my mailbox. Struggling to extricate a plume of junk mail, I froze at the peripheral sighting of a familiar figure's shadow passing behind me; I turned in time to register his profile. Channing's observation confirmed: "His face, once seen, could not be forgotten."

Without a plan, I pursued wisdom; increasing my pace to a sprint, I arrived at his side calmly inquiring, "Mr. Thoreau, might I join you for your saunter?"

Receiving approval, I burst forth, "It's a shipwreck; we are drowning and wresting each other's plank! The gizzard of society, its opposite halves — our two political parties — are now grinding relentlessly on each other. Anger, fear, hatred, misogyny, racism, and prejudice are the grit and gravel shoveled into an overflowing public feeding trough — by the media!"

Words unminced, he responded: "Have you heard the gurgling of the sewer through every column? I contend the press… live and rule only by their servility, and appealing to the worst, and not the better nature of man, the people who read them are in the condition of the dog that returns to his vomit."

I thought for a moment. Would he consider FOX wastewater and Breitbart regurgitation — or vice versa?

Shamelessly I asked, knowing the answer, "Time to make another donation to NPR and PBS — right?"

Unfazed by the acronyms, he replied, "Remember truth is stronger than error."

My barrage continued: "Our democracy has been profoundly corrupted by money. The Supreme Court has ruled to grant certain rights of the individual to corporations!"

A tad annoyed at having to state the obvious, he uttered, "It is truly enough said, that a corporation has no conscience... Unjust laws exist: shall we be content to obey them, or shall we endeavor to amend them, and obey them until we have succeeded, or shall we transgress them at once?"

"Maybe a mix of obey and transgress?" I timidly queried.

He shot back: "How does it become a man to behave toward the American government to-day? I answer that he cannot without disgrace be associated with it."

I got it; time to transgress.

"And Henry, of dire consequence for all living species is climate change. Human pollution is warming our planet at an alarming rate. The new administration calls the science behind global warming a hoax. They are backing out of international treaties to curb greenhouse gasses and have repealed emission regulations."

He warned, "Most men do not care for Nature.... we need to protect all from the vandalism of a few."

His eyebrows arched, registering the reality and sadness of my disclosure that societal and environmental vandalism had grown exponentially since the 19th century.

He kindly rallied, "Let every man make known what kind of

government would command his respect, and that will be one step toward obtaining it."

My last question: "What about the children? They spend countless hours indoors — tethered to computer screens. Depression is our new epidemic."

Catching sight of a bluebird, he offered up the prescription: "Nature is but another word for health... There can be no black melancholy to him who lives in the midst of Nature and has his senses still."

It was time to take my leave and allow him the stillness he had sought. I thanked him profusely, turned, and started to jog back towards obligations, still anxiously contemplating the plethora of challenges; he sensed my lingering despair and called out to me:

"I came into this world, not chiefly to make it a good place to live in, but to live in it, be it good or bad. A man has not everything to do, but to do something..."

At that moment, I found myself free — free to do something, *not* everything. Walking back into the woods, I lightened my steps, stilled my senses, listened for the crickets, and made my way to the huckleberry field on one of the highest hills.

I slept well that night — ready to awaken.

Photo credit: Susan Wilson

Jeff Zinn is a director and actor. He is the managing director of Gloucester Stage Company in Gloucester, Massachusetts and the author of The Existential Actor: Life and Death, Onstage and Off. *His father was the historian and social critic Howard Zinn.*

Desperate Heroes

Jeff Zinn

As actors approach playing a given role, they are always trying to figure out the *action* of the character. Superseding the cliché question, "What's my motivation," we ask, "What is the character doing in any given moment?" In life, each of us constructs an identity that protects us from existential dread. It follows that as we go about our lives, a primary action we engage in is the construction and defense of that death-denying identity.

In my book, *The Existential Actor: Life & Death, Onstage & Off,* I talk about how, since both actors and the characters they play share this driving motivation, awareness of how we negotiate the heroic narrative of our own lives can help us play characters quite different from ourselves.

In a very real way, all of us are actors — and heroes. Everyone is playing the leading role in the story of his or her own life, the heroic narrative in which each of us is the protagonist. The classical hero goes into battle, faces death, and survives. Compared with the exploits of, say, Achilles, simply surviving our day-to-day existence might seem an egregious lowering of the heroism bar.

Henry David Thoreau wrote, "Most men lead lives of quiet desperation," which doesn't sound especially heroic. But all of us, even in our quietest shapes, are living heroically, or trying to. We must.

Awareness of death can elicit a kind of stage fright. What if you believed — not just intellectually, but viscerally — that right outside your door the chances were even that a sniper would fire at you from a hidden vantage point, a car would run you down, a passing meteor would veer off course and smash into the earth, annihilating not just you but all of life? The result would be paralysis, a sense of being frozen in the wings, rendering you unable to step out onto the stages of your life.

The solution, according to Ernest Becker and others, is to wrap ourselves in layers of psychological armor. Culture provides that armor: a ready-made framework, a worldview complete with rules for how to walk, talk, dress, and behave. Each culture generates its own versions of these things and communicates them to its members in a million ways: parent to child, peer to peer, through educational systems, and through the media.

The roles we adopt, the way we walk and talk and behave, the groups we join, the teams we root for — a package of attributes I call *shape* — help us shield ourselves from the terrible truth of existence. These shapes allow us to act — to move forward with agency and without paralysis. Throughout our lives we all cling to our heroic narratives, whether modest or grandiose. We drive cars, live in houses, go shopping, and educate our children. It is right and fitting that we do so. The paradox of psychological health is that to function with any equilibrium at all, we must engage in a vital lie; we must deny the fact of our mortality. Ironically, mental health may require shutting out the truth. Mental health may require us to narrow down our capacity for feeling everything. Mental health may require us not to surrender to the awful truth of our cosmic insignificance.

Every day we get out of bed and we act. I don't mean that we put on a show or pretend anything. I mean that we take action. We do. According to Jean Paul Sartre, we only exist through what we do.

He said, "There is no reality except in action. Man is nothing but the sum of his actions. ... There is no love apart from the deeds of love; there is no genius other than that which is expressed in works of art."

The idea is ancient. Karma is the Sanskrit word for action. You are what you do. You become what you do. You are who you are because of what you've done.

Thoreau challenges us to choose our psychological armor carefully. We can walk through life straitjacketed, or we can wear the armor more lightly, more deliberately.

Write at a replica of the desk Thoreau had at Walden Pond.

Write Your Next Work in Thoreau's Birth Room!

"Write while the heat is in you. The writer who postpones the recording of his thoughts uses an iron which has cooled to burn a hole with. He cannot inflame the minds of his audience." — Henry David Thoreau

The Thoreau Farm Writers Retreat is a perfect, bucolic setting for writers who wish uninterrupted concentration and a reprieve from urban stress.

It was in this room in this house that Henry David Thoreau was born on July 12, 1817, and where his friend Ellery Channing wrote, "He first saw the light" and "drew his first breath in a pure country air, out of crowded towns, amid the pleasant russet fields."

The historic house and its immediate surroundings have been restored to the look and feel of Thoreau's time. The site is listed on the National Register of Historic Places and in 2012 won a Massachusetts Preservation Award.

Our Thoreau Farm Writers Retreat may be rented for a $150 per day donation; $75 for members of Thoreau Farm. Although lodging is not available at the farmhouse, accommodations can be found in nearby Concord. All donations support the upkeep and educational programming of Thoreau Farm.

Email us at info@thoreaufarm.org or call 978.451.0300 to learn more or to make a reservation today.

Made in the USA
Columbia, SC
27 September 2018